The Country Schoolteacher
A KANSAS LEGACY

Cover Photo - Ellen Stacey, Pardee School, Atchison County

A Collection of Memories
Compiled and edited by Vera Ellerman Rodecap

ISBN 0-9639944-0-9

Printed in the United States of America
by Bell Graphics, Holton, Kansas
Fourth Printing
February 1995

Table of Contents

Chapter Two Cont.

Acknowledgements

with special thanks. . . .

to all who shared their memories of teaching in the Kansas one-room schools

to Dr. Allan Miller, Fort Hays State University

to Dr. Roy Sheldon, Washburn University Writing Center

to Dan Fitzgerald, Kansas State Historical Society

to Peggy Wolivar, Topeka, for her typing skills

to my family and friends for their constant encouragement

Introduction

I remember my grandfather's stories — his many tales of growing up in rural Kansas. As he got older, his stories drifted back further and further in his life, past his World War I enlistment day or the dark days when the dust storms obscured even the faintest candlelight just inches from his face. My grandfather was a man who had witnessed many events in the early twentieth century, yet his mind seemed to focus on school life. Sure, not all of his stories, like many things told a hundred fold, were now historically accurate. Yet, we grandkids didn't care about that. We liked the way he told them.

My grandfather took a great deal of pride when it came to "book learnin." True, he had made it only through the eighth grade but somehow he had developed a keen sense of knowledge, rare even among the finest of college graduates. His ivy-covered hall of learning was not a marble monolith constructed out of the finest of stone. Instead, it was a simple wooden one-room schoolhouse barely a quarter of a mile away. It was one giant room where all kids of all age groups gathered to learn from one another, a "team effort." My grandfather was in charge of keeping the pot-bellied stove fired up during the winter and keeping the blackboards clean during the spring. When he was not studying his own grade level, he was eavesdropping on another. This method saved time; if a student was smart and innovative, he could theoretically work his way through the lessons of all the grades in a single year! Most of all, he loved the outdoor games, games which have disappeared — red rover, fox and geese, hopscotch to name a few. He made education seem like such innocent fun coupled with a moderate amount of hard work. Perhaps in his day it was. When my grandfather passed away, he took those memories with him, and now the stories, which were never recorded at the time, are quickly fading from memory.

Now, years later, my daughter is starting school for the first time. There are no one-room country schools for her. There are no grades beyond her own, only walls that separate her from the other classes that appear to be just beyond her reach. The hallways are cold and stark, the sunlight a far different color as it reflects off the simulated wood paneling in each of the rooms. Not only do they teach reading, writing, and simple math, but now they throw in helpful hints of psychoanalysis, as well as mysterious tests that predict the outcome of a child's educational career before they can even write their own name. Somewhere, somehow, life has become far too complex. It has moved beyond the primary goal of education and into the realm of realistic absurdity.

In search of our roots, I am proud to present to the reader this volume which takes all of us back to the beginnings of education, back to the days of the one-room country school. For older readers, this will be a yearbook of sorts. The reminiscences included here will allow some to travel back to their school days, to a much more simpler era. For those of us who did not experience this, the accounts on the following pages will enlighten us regarding what education is all about, and perhaps guide us down the roads where it diverged into something else.

How did education in Kansas begin? What were the goals of the one-room country school system? The following stories will unlock some of these secrets.

Public eduction in Kansas was a primary concern of the citizens as soon as the land was open for settlement in 1854. Communities were instructed to provide schools in any manner possible. In Lawrence, for example, the first school was held in a room in the New England Emigrant Aid building. It would be several years before more permanent quarters would be established. The first territorial legislature in 1855 created the office of county superintendent of public instruction and gave this official the power to create and alter school districts. The legislature of 1858 provided for district school boards of three members to be elected at an annual meeting and to serve for three year terms. Every school was to offer instruction in orthography (spelling), reading, writing, English grammar, geography, arithmetic, and any other subjects which the board deemed appropriate. By 1859, two hundred twenty school districts had been organized.

Despite the high priority the state placed on public education, pioneer conditions prevailed during the first few decades of statehood. In Pawnee County in 1873, school was held in a former saloon where the teacher used the bar as a desk. Books were whatever the students brought from home. As late as 1917, Maude Elliott, a teacher in rural

Finney County, taught class in a converted shoe shop. Conditions for education were much more advanced in the towns and established farm communities. By the late 1860's, substantial and architecturally impressive buildings were constructed in Atchison, Topeka, and Leavenworth. In rural areas where building materials were readily available, handsome one-room schoolhouses of wood, brick, and stone were erected. By 1908, the state had 8,689 organized school districts. More than three-fourths of these were rural, one-room schools. Although not every district held school every year, most districts were active. As Kansans entered the twentieth century, eight grades of schooling were available to most, but high school education was still confined to towns and cities.

The quality of education varied markedly from district to district. This disturbed state school officials, who believed that quality education should be available to everyone. At first, attention was focused on the qualifications of the teachers. An 1874 report on education stated that only one in four teachers was actually qualified to educate children. Soon, a system of examination and certification was established to assure that Kansas was getting only the best qualified teachers. In the first two decades of the twentieth century, however, many state educators believed that the entire educational system was in need of reform, and in 1916, the Kansas State Department of Education published a pamphlet on standards specifically for rural schools. Some of the standards stressed included the kind of certification held by the teacher, the teacher's years of experience, and the professional attitude of the teacher. Certain physical aspects of the rural schools was also stressed. Every one-room school needed a good water supply, adequate toilets, a flag and flagpole, three pieces of playground equipment, a school building in good repair, satisfactory lighting, heat and ventilation. Standard teaching aids included fifty volumes of suitable books, two full sets of supplementary readers, maps, globes, and a dictionary. Two supervisors were employed to inspect rural schools. The state department compiled records of those schools visited and produced a map showing the location of schools which received a standard rating.

Despite these efforts, most rural schools did not achieve the standards set forth. In 1916, of the 792 schools visited, only 119 in 67 counties were approved as standard schools. While some school districts sought to improve and standardize, too many of them chose to ignore many of the state recommendations. Many professional educators seemed almost embarrassed by rural schools. A movement toward school district consolidation began which would eliminate the numerous small districts and transform them into larger, more controllable entities. State educators, such as C.E. Rarick, stated as early as 1923 that the one-teacher school system had outlived its usefulness. C.V. Williams wrote, in a supplement to the textbook ***Human Geography,*** that "A good way to judge the people of a community is by their schools. In an agricultural state like ours one might expect to see old-fashioned, one-room country schools with rusty stoves and dingy water pails. Too many of this kind of schools continue to exist in our state, but they are giving way to well-equipped modern buildings."

Consolidation was slow in coming. Many smaller districts refused to give up their local school for a larger one several miles away. In 1909, Kansas had forty-four consolidated school districts out of more than seven thousand rural districts. After the state began setting school standards six years later, the pressure to consolidate schools increased. Educators became relentless in their efforts to modernize and upgrade the rural schools. Nearly every speech at every state educational meeting was full of negative, blistering attacks on the state of rural education in Kansas. School textbooks, such as Anna Arnold's ***Civics and Citizenship*** were unfair and insulting: "In rural districts the schools are often poorly organized. Pupils of all ages and grades are in the same room, and usually the number of classes is so large that only a few minutes can be given to each recitation. In many cases the district can not afford an experienced teacher and the building and equipment is poor. The schools are often so small as to be lacking in interest and life. . . . The rural school has not kept up with the general progress of the times."

Many educators took their consolidation plans on the road. They met with school districts all over that state in an attempt to encourage them to consolidate. The consolidation movement caught on slowly, especially when finances were discussed. School districts were sold on the fact that financing larger but fewer districts would be less expensive and better utilized than maintaining the smaller districts. The move to bring districts together began in the 1920's, slowed in the depression years of the 1930's, and accelerated rapidly after World War II. By the 1960s, the last of the one room schools ceased to exist and the office of county superintendent, which once oversaw this vast network of independent learning centers, was abolished, the records being merged with the county register of deeds.

The rural schools brought basic education to a rapidly expanding population at a time when land and economic opportunities seemed to be unlimited. In spite of their shortcomings, most students received more personal attention than their consolidated counterparts. There were, however, vast inequalities among these rural schools. Schools could not and were not expected to serve pupils with disabilities or special needs or to solve social problems. The progressive education movement, however, which had the goal of social improvement, encouraged the remodeling of many rural school buildings and the addition of practical courses to the curriculum.

Today, the one-room schools of Kansas have met many fates. Many have been abandoned, some have been adapted for farm use, a few have been converted to family homes, and fewer still have been preserved as museums or community buildings. The fate of many of the communities around these little schools has also been devastating. These one-room schools were the social centers of many rural communities. When the schools were abolished due to consolidation, the social network of people who used the school as a gathering place was broken. Our great educational experts were quick to espouse the advantages of consolidated school districts, but failed to look at the impact the local school had on its community. In many cases, when one disappeared, so did the other.

When I look back and read the speeches made regarding how many disadvantages our ancestors had in being educated in the one - room school, it is a wonder that they could function at all in society. However, many of the byproducts of a one-room country school not only functioned, but excelled. My grandfather could do complex mathematical equations in his head; now we have to use a calculator. He could break apart the structure of a sentence into the appropriate verbs, nouns, and adjectives. Today many of us are lucky to be able to write a sentence. He drew up blueprints to build his second farmhouse from a pile of timbers, and the house stood sixty years. I could not even do that with a masters degree from college. The one-room country schools may have failed the tests of standardization, but they educated their pupils. . . and that is the true test of success.

I know the readers will enjoy the reminiscences that follow. Each one documents a different experience that will add to our collective knowledge of our ancestors and the values that were important to them. . . values which have disappeared or which have been drastically altered.

I had hopes that my six year old daughter would have the opportunity to visit her great-grandfather's one-room country school. It was one of the survivors, one of the few structures left unaltered in the middle of a wind-swept Kansas wheat field. Such will not be the case, however, as the building burned to the ground a week before her first day of school.

In life, the art of learning is so important. Our world changes so quickly that we do not take time out to study the impact of these changes and how they will affect future generations. This book is a part of that learning experience; it is an important testimonial concerning perhaps the best remembered years of our lives — those carefree school days when each day was sweet and worries were few. Those were the years that were gone in the blink of an eye, but stay with us the rest of our lives.

Daniel C. Fitzgerald

Foreword

No other institution has shaped Kansas character more than the country one-room school. Everything serves its purpose and moves on. So it is with the one-room school concept and its teacher. The small square sentinels of learning are now converted to dwellings, farm storage buildings or are simply left to rot away on some remote road. The remaining teachers are retired, teaching in our present system or on to more lucrative vocations.

I think many other Kansans share my love of the one-room school. The waves of nostalgia wash over us as we remember those days whether it be as a student or a teacher. I was fortunate enough to have been in both positions. I attended Hickory Grove School, located on the Jefferson-Atchison County line about 4 miles west of Nortonville, Kansas. We called it "Sugar Bowl" School. Many rural schools had nicknames. Ours was called "Sugar Bowl" because it was told someone had stolen the sugar bowl at one of the school's potluck dinners.

I'll never forget the excitement of my first day of school. That wonderful smell of musty books, sweeping compound and the gentle breeze blowing in the open windows will always be with me. I attended that school with my sisters and cousins for seven years. I skipped the eighth grade and took the county exam to enter high school with my cousin. If you had mastered the curriculum, this was a common practice.

My preparation for teaching was 60 hours credit from Highland Junior College with no student teaching as we know it today. I was 19 years old when I signed my first contract. I had married the previous spring and was expecting my first child in January. Knowing I would have to take some time off to give birth, I asked the three farmers on the board for $2200 for the eight month term. Some teachers were getting as high as $3000 in the 1950's. Teachers were scarce then and they hired me with the understanding my sister would substitute for me when needed. This school was Star School, District 73, located a few miles north-east of Nortonville in Atchison County. The student body consisted of nine students in six grades. Two of the boys were children of one of my grade school teachers.

I felt the same anticipation and excitement when the first day arrived, this time as the teacher. I couldn't wait to get the key and open the school house. That wonderful combination of smells met me at the door and somehow gave me the confidence that I could teach.

The memories are so warm from that teaching experience that I wanted to share and help preserve that era of education. The idea of collecting memories from other one-room school teachers kept coming to me persistently as I realized the day will come when this first hand accounting will no longer be available.

I first started this project by asking my former teachers and others who had taught in the Kansas one-room schools for their memories and experiences. Word spread and soon I was receiving wonderful letters and tapes. Later, I devised a short questionnaire that asked for a few facts, such as the location of the school, nickname and the type of certification the teacher held.

The correspondence has been priceless. Some letters were written with great difficulty due to poor eyesight, physical problems and advanced age. The common thread among all the letters was the love of teaching and the warmth radiated from every contribution. These teachers made this effort because they knew the importance of this preservation.

I kept the letters intact as I felt they lost feeling by being dissected into subjects, locations, or other common themes. Some memories are taken from taped interviews. I have strived for integrity in transcribing them into their stories.

On the following pages, memories unfold to give us a nostalgic picture of our educational heritage.

Vera Ellerman Rodecap

Atchison County

Star School, District 73, Atchison County
Students, 1954-55

My first day as a teacher

Chapter One

One-room schools flourished during the late teens and through the 20's. It wasn't unusual for a teacher to be hired with only an 8th grade education and as young as 16 or 17 years old.

It was the time of World War I, and teachers mention planting Victory gardens and being sick with the Spanish influenza. A variety of natural hazards plagued the country schoolteachers, and they tell of tall snowdrifts, blizzards, flooding, and dust storms. Most schools were without a telephone, and the teachers and students had to be prepared for difficult times. Transportation to and from school was by horseback, horse and buggy, or walking. Automobiles in this early time were undependable, and roads often impassable in inclement weather. Eliza Atkinson tells of living for a time in the schoolhouse with an oil stove and cot as her only comforts of home. Teachers lived at home if they were lucky enough to get a school close by. It was more common for them to board with families in the community. They helped with the evening chores and attended church on Sunday with the family. They ate with the family and learned to eat the unfamiliar. They tell of drinking goat's milk and eating pie for breakfast.

Enrollment was as high as 30 to 40 students in all 8 grades. Some students were as old as the teacher and many attended sporadically due to having to help with harvests and the chores at home.

Most rural teachers in this time kept order with the "hickory stick" theory of discipline. Progressive teachers in the cities, who bought the beliefs of educator John Dewey, did away with corporal punishments. The more modern teachers at first referred to these rural teachers as "hickory" people. By World War I talkers shortened the durable word in size and significance to "hick." Unfortunately, this nickname still is used at times to describe country people and small towns in Kansas.

The curriculum consisted of the basic 3 R's, but also included Agriculture and Geography. Teaching Agriculture was a big challenge to some of the city girls teaching in the country. If high school wasn't a possibility, some girls would return for a ninth year to help the teacher and to gain a little more schooling.

Box suppers were a popular source of entertainment, with the teacher's box going for a premium price.

The school was the center of community activity, providing a place for dances and even church services.

The school was the cement that held the community together through many Kansas hardships.

Wichita County
Conquest School
1915

County Superintendent and Teacher at the Same Time

Eliza Atkinson
from an interview by Billie L. Biel
courtesy of Fort Hays State University

I started teaching in 1915. At that time you wouldn't have to have but an 8th grade education if you could pass the teacher's examination. Most of the teachers at the time I taught did not have any high school at all. Some of the teachers when I first started were teaching in sod schoolhouses. The last sod schoolhouse in the county was during the time I was County Superintendent.

When I ran out of a place to stay they let me take a small bed and a 3 burner oil stove into the building and I batched, so to speak. Had to go across over to Mr. Higgins to get my water and so on. Carried it across.

The first time I was appointed County Superintendent, I had a school and I talked it over with the school board, and they allowed me to send a substitute out on Monday, so I kept the office open. It was to be open two days a week. I kept it open on Saturday and Monday and taught school the rest of the week.

I had a deaf boy in one school. He had learned to talk before he went deaf. I think he had the measles and the whooping cough at the same time and that caused him to lose his hearing. He was a lip reader. I stood in front of his desk and pronounced his spelling words to him when he'd look up at me, so we got along fine. Later on, he went to Washington, D.C. to the deaf school, and he teaches in a deaf college somewhere.

Pie for Breakfast

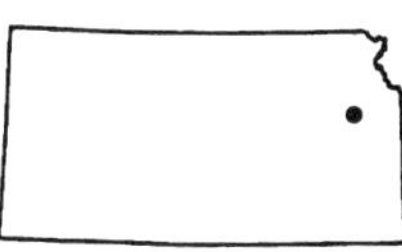

Douglas County
Worden School

Helen Jackson Hamilton
as told to her daughter, Janet Ogan, Topeka, Kansas

In 1916, my mother, Helen Jackson Hamilton was given her first job as a teacher. She was 20 years old. For preparation, she had one semester at Kansas University and one summer session at Pittsburg Normal (now Pittsburg State University).

The school was located in the small town of Worden in Douglas county about 20 miles southwest of Lawrence. She rented a room in the home of a Dunkard family by the name of Laughlin. This house was one block from the school. The lady of the house served pie for breakfast every morning, even if she had to bake her pies at night. My mother gained 25 pounds that year. Room and board cost $15.00 a month.

Not only was she the teacher of thirty students, but she was also the custodian. She had to get to school by 8:00 A.M. to start the wood burning stove which heated the building. The small children who walked two or three miles to school were thoroughly chilled by the time they arrived. Otherwise, transportation was by horse and buggy.

She was expected to keep the building clean. The School Superintendent visited her school one day and when he found the boys' outhouse dirty, he told her to get it cleaned up. She had checked the girls' outhouse but not the boys'. She asked the boys to bring buckets and do it after school. They cleaned it well and kept it that way after that.

She taught the usual subjects of Reading, English, Spelling, and Mathematics plus Agriculture, which she had to study diligently before class, since she had always lived in the city. She was responsible for grades one through nine. The front row of students would work with her while the rest did their lessons assigned. There were two girls in the eighth grade who had tried to pass the examinations to enter high school. They had tried for three years. After her year of working with them, they finally passed.

The children and teacher brought their lunches and ate together at noon. When it was cold enough, they would all go ice skating, which they enjoyed at a nearby little creek.

The parents of the students took turns inviting the teacher to their homes for dinner. Sometimes they had box suppers at school for social gatherings.

She would go home to Kansas City on weekends sometimes. She would board a train eight miles away at Baldwin. The young men would vie for the privilege to drive her in their horse and buggy to the depot.

Her salary was $50.00 a month. At the end of the year, she was offered a raise of $20.00 per month if she would return there to teach next year. However, she was offered $70.00 per month to teach 3rd and 4th grades in Eudora, Kansas. She accepted that position.

She enjoyed that year of teaching at Worden and has happy memories of that experience.

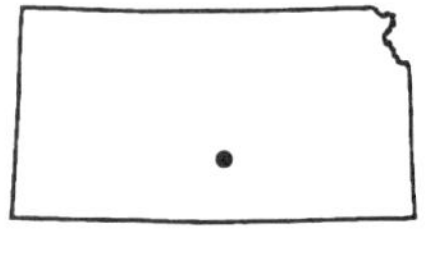

Reno County

Homemade Paste Spoils and Other Happenings

Gladys Lauver

Nickerson, Kansas

Ireton, Dist. 63, 7 month term, 1916-17
Enterprise, Dist. 122, 1917-20
Castleton, 1920-22
Nickerson Grade School, 1924-63

Drinking water came from a pump in the school yard. Imagine on a cold wintery day filling a bucket to bring into the schoolhouse. Coal was carried in and stored around the stove to be used as needed. Big boys usually did that, and the hot ashes were carried out by me at the end of the day. Then I laid the fire for the next day, swept the floor and put everything in order for the following day. Then I walked two miles to my boarding place, or sometimes I had a ride during a blizzard.

One of our teachers was fired because she married during the school term. Another taboo was going into the barber shop to have my bobbed hair trimmed. I felt very uncomfortable and out of place.

Since I had to furnish my own supplies in the one-room school, I cooked a batch of paste at home and carried it back with me. One time during hot weather it spoiled and had to be discarded - quite a loss!

When I first visited my second school, I hired a friend to take me and my supplies to the building, a few days before school. When we arrived, the building was locked, so I crawled through the only unlocked window and left my boxes there. One time on my arrival at school, the skunks had crawled through an opening into the basement and we had to go home until they left.

Lunches were cold and brought into the schoolroom in winter. Toilets were out of doors, separated as far as possible. A cold trip on a wintery day!

During my first year of teaching, I earned $50.00 per month, paid $16.00 for board and room, and felt rich indeed with that $34.00. To get my check I walked to the farm homes of three board members, 1 mile east and return, 1/2 mile south and return. Then the third one was a little closer.

It was during this year, 1916-1917, that tragedy entered our home in Nickerson with the death of an older sister. My father drove the 20-plus miles in a horse and buggy to take me home for a few days. This sadness, homesickness, and teaching experience helped me prepare for adulthood.

In the spring of 1919, during World War I, the pupils and I planted a Victory garden in a small part of the school yard. I didn't have a chance to see it grow. When I went home for the weekend, I awoke the next morning with the Spanish influenza and was not able to finish the school year. However, the pupils living nearby enjoyed the results of their labor.

Dust bowl days and the depression were sad and troublesome

times. My salary was reduced from $100.00 a month in 1925-26 to $90.00 in 1926-27. It was a struggle for my mother and I to stay out of debt. In fact, we were a bit hungry at times. Nobody complained of outdated clothes and runners in hose, since all of us were in the same predicament. School was dismissed early one day because of the ominous dust cloud that obscured the sun. Parents and other adults took children home safely. I held the hands of children coming my way until they reached their homes. By the time I arrived at home, dust like snow settled on my shoulders and glasses. During this time, the new banker absconded with the funds, and left the town in dire circumstances.

World War II took not only fathers, but also mothers out of the home. As a result, older children were responsible for younger ones. Home studies were neglected and family life declined. Today we can see the results of this change in the lawless actions, lack of moral training and irresponsible actions of some of the present generation.

The Reno County Superintendent of Schools issued certificates to those who passed the test. Those who had the highest scores received a certificate for three years, the next group for two years and the lowest score, 1 year. My first two certificates were for two years each. Then I took the state exams and received one for five years, renewed, and received a permanent Normal Training Certificate, which I used until I retired in 1963.

HOMEMADE SCHOOL PASTE

1 cup Sugar
1 tablespoon Powdered Alum
1 cup Flour
1 quart water
30 drops of Oil of Cloves

Mix and cook in a double boiler until clear like starch. Remove from fire and add Oil of Cloves.

LIBRARY PASTE

1 cup Flour
1 tablespoon Alum
1 quart Water
10 drops of Oil of Cloves

Bring water and alum to the boiling point. Add flour which has been mixed with a portion of water to a smooth paste. Boil in a double boiler for 20 minutes. Add Oil of Cloves and strain through a sieve. This keeps indefinitely.

Too Much to Eat

Mary Vincent Ellerman
Nortonville, Kansas
Clingan - 1923-24

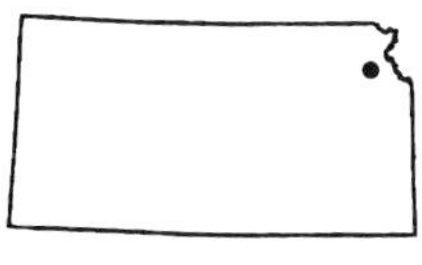

Atchison County

I taught Clingan School in Atchison County in 1923-24. I boarded with Jack and Hazel Keirns. Hazel put up big lunches and I never could eat it all so I would put it under a loose floor board on the porch of the school. I figure I fed the rats pretty well. Jack was always pulling some joke on me. One evening I was asleep in my chair and my mouth was open and he put quinine in my mouth. I could have killed him!

Of course I had all the classes to teach and all the other work to be done. One time at recess I fell against a barbed wire fence and cut my arm and got a bad infection.

I had to walk about a mile to school. This was my first experience teaching black students, the Boldridge family. They came to see me after I quit teaching there.

I got my education at Milton College, Milton, Wisconsin, Emporia State University and Mount St. Scholastica College in Atchison, Kansas. I had enough hours for a degree but never applied for it.

Borrowed a Shirt and got a Husband

Ruth Barnes Sims
Kansas City, Kansas

Linn County
Miami County

Linn County — *Twin Springs School - 1928-29*
Miami County
Sunny Ridge, District 59 - 1929-31
Lone Elm, District 63 - 1931-36
Substitute teaching in Johnson County, 1949-56

In August, 1928, I began my maiden voyage as a rural school teacher. I was staying in Paola, as we lived in a rural community too far to drive daily — plus the fact I had not learned to drive my father's 1919 Dodge Touring car when I attended my first institute. I was told that on Thursday evening the teachers had a picnic in Wallace Park following a baseball game of lady teachers against the men teachers. I had not been told that previously and had always been a tomboy. I really wanted to play but did not have my knickers with me. A close friend said she was sure I could wear her brother's pants — but what about a shirt? Just then a handsome young man, who had been outside the office door eaves-dropping, walked in and said, "I just bought four new white shirts. You may wear one of them." I didn't know him, but he had taught for four years and I assumed he had money. I weighed about one hundred pounds, and this character weighed one-hundred eighty-seven and was five feet, eleven inches tall. What an opportunity! As he always told the story, he loaned me his shirt, and I wore the pants for four years of courtship and 57¹/₂ years of a beautiful, loving marriage.

The rural school marathon began in September, 1928, following words of wisdom from the School Board Director, who called and said, "You are hired". My first school had 20 children, all ages except the fifth. Two of the group were from an orphanage in New York and lived in a home that made them work very hard and mistreated them. Two students were from a divorced home, and that created a problem. The other sixteen were from average to above average homes. I had to prove myself in September when they brought me a "woolyworm", just like our instructor at Institute had told us. Yes, I held it and that got rid of that fun, but I really put up a front.

In the spring, when the ground was still frozen underneath but thawed on top, I tore the ligaments loose in my knee kicking a football. The kids brought a little wagon to school and pulled me around the school yard, as they would not play without me.

Outside the regular curriculum was the yearly program and box supper. The children gave dialogues, readings, musical numbers, etc. in the evening for relatives and friends. The girls, women, and teachers took a box decorated in crepe paper and filled with goodies to eat. An auctioneer would sell them — your fellow would buy them and the teacher's boyfriend would buy hers. My "lover boy" had an agreement for a fixed amount, and then he would drop off on the other guy.

Usually several others would have to pool their money to the other guy. Those were the good old days of the early thirties and the Great Depression.

The last year that I taught I went home and stayed all night with seven of the eight families in the school. What an award to receive!

The county superintendent visited the school once a year. You never knew when she might drop in. She came to our school between the first recess and noon. As the children went out to eat their lunch she visited with me. When I escorted her to the door, the boys had "tinned canned" a stray dog that was outside. Embarrassed? Yes, but she was a farmer's daughter and shared in their fun in spite of my wanting to crawl in a hole. Two of these boys are now auctioneers. They smile from their platform if they see me now and give me a big hug. They are now in their 60's. I just turn to my friends and say, "I always kiss the auctioneers when I go to a sale." I think that is another reward for being a rural school teacher.

On one occasion my husband and I went to a box supper in a school where we had both taught in years gone by. As the auctioneer was selling boxes, a girl whom I had in the second and third grade stepped out from behind the curtain, and I waved to her. The auctioneer said, "Sold to the young lady in the back seat." My husband got a big bang out of that, and I learned a lesson. Never wave to anyone at a sale. You might buy something you don't want.

The memories grow fonder
For years back yonder,
The joy in the one-room school
Brings happiness and today we can say
Wasn't it, or isn't it cool?

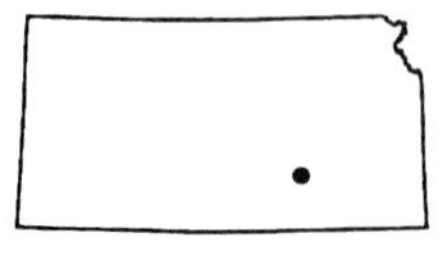

Greenwood County

Advice to the Lovelorn and Other Challenges

Mary E. Akey Hogan
Hamilton, Kansas

District 77, near Madison - 1924-25
District 1, near Madison - 1927-28
Willow Valley District 16 near Hamilton - 1928-31
Prairie Breeze #24 near Hamilton - 1957-61

While teaching in 1927, I remember one father that came to see me to discuss his little girl's school work. He spent most of the time discussing whether he should marry his housekeeper. His wife had died. He had a small boy at home and the little girl at school. He did marry the housekeeper and I guess my advice must have been right. It seemed to work out well. He was a man several years older than me. I certainly didn't feel qualified to give him advice.

Another time I remember a terrific wind, rain and hail storm. A windowpane blew out of a window letting in a lot of water. The children were very frightened. There were about ten in the school. I gathered them around me and read until it became so dark I couldn't see. One little girl asked me to pray, which I did. Eventually the storm passed. Debris was spread over fields and a small building blew away. Yes, I was scared, too! Both of the above events happened at the same school in Madison, Kansas in the year 1927-28.

I think the saddest time was in Willow Valley School in the Hamilton community. That was the death of one of my little girl's mother at the birth of a child. I also remember another incident at the same school. In those days the teacher was the janitor and I needed kindling to start a fire. I told the school board and one of them brought a load of old boards. Now they had to be cut up to make kindling size. My attempt to cut them ended with one board flying up and cutting a gash in my forehead. The next evening this same man came to pick up his little girl after school. I was waiting for him. I told him I needed the boards cut up. I said that my education did not include cutting wood. I showed him my cut forehead. The next day he cut my kindling. I expect he told the neighbors and had a good laugh over the teacher who couldn't cut kindling.

While teaching the four school terms at Prairie Breeze, District 16, close to Hamilton (1957-61), the school board made it possible for the school to take several trips. One year we went to Hutchinson to the State Fair. Another year we went to Woolroc (?), Oklahoma. The attendance at this school was usually between twelve and fifteen. One morning a mother came by and told us there was a large flock of geese on their way north. They were in a neighbor's milo field. We piled the students into her car and mine and went to see them. That was the largest flock of wild geese any of us had ever seen. The noise was terrific. This was an interesting as well as an educational event for the children. This school was not close to any large body of water, so geese did not stay for more than one day and night.

Students Became Stepsons

Delphine Sinel Leonard
Topeka, Kansas

Shawnee County
Osage County
1928-48

Shawnee
Six Mile, Lyons, Lone Tree, Vidette, Matney
Osage
Kinneyville , Glenwood

My first school in 1928 was Six Mile School, very close to my home. I drove my first car and had a little neighbor boy ride with me. I had 28 pupils in all eight grades. It was quite a challenge! One event I had that year was a box supper, which was quite popular at schools in those years. One boy, I guess, was determined to buy my box so some of the other boys kept bidding against him until he had to pay $20.00 for it.

My next school was Lyons, east of Berryton. I don't remember how many pupils I had but among them were three boys who much later became my stepsons. I remember one of these boys said that I had eyes in the back of my head. None of my students got away with much mischief.

Kinneyville in Osage County was my next school. I had a very large attendance and all eight grades. I taught there for four years. I met some wonderful people in all those years. I boarded with a prominent rancher and his family and learned to play bridge with them. I have forgotten by now.

My next school was Glenwood which was near Kinneyville. One thing I remember about this place where I stayed was that I learned to drink goat's milk. The couple who stood up with my husband and me when we got married were very close friends and a prominent family in the neighborhood. One of my pupils was their daughter. When it was time to review for the 8th grade exams, we studied outdoors in the shade of the beautiful trees.

Lone Tree, near Dover, was my next school. Discipline in my schools was no problem, but I did have to send one of the younger boys home one day. My words meant much in discipline!

Here I drove a horse and buggy with two of the children where I boarded. If it was very stormy the man took us to school.

One of the best loved schools that I taught was Vidette, not far from Lone Tree. I stayed with a lovely older couple who were so good to me. They made me feel so "at home". When the weather was good I walked to and from school. On the way I had to pass a pasture that had a fierce looking "Ferdinand". I always made it but I was rather afraid. At this home I met my husband. One day while I was teaching class, some one knocked at the door. When I opened the door there he stood and was I surprised! I had known of him from another school I taught. This was in April and we were engaged the following October.

My last year was at Matney, north of "Old Richland". We were married in May, 1944 and I retired in 1948. It was the beginning of consolidation. The school was closed permanently in 1948 and ended up with four pupils and four grades.

I always played ball wherever I taught and was often chosen as pitcher. I so enjoyed the children! I tried to have three programs a year, Halloween, Christmas and the last day of school. I carried many buckets of coal and ashes, swept many floors, dusted many erasers, washed many blackboards and put up many flags.

Several of my former pupils have died, some have gone on to good jobs. Many have remembered me in the past years. I wouldn't take anything for all my years of teaching experience. Sixty-two years have gone by since I began!

Matney School

Troubled Kids

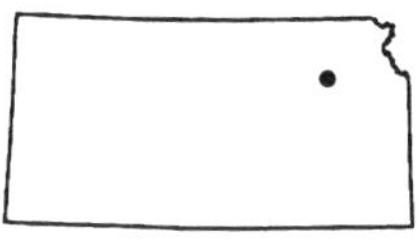

Shawnee County

Mrs. Ruth Marken

Topeka, Kansas

Fairview School, Decker School, Sunbeam School, Union School

I graduated from Seaman High School in the spring of 1922. Our home was in the Fairview District. My mother was on the school board at the time. The other two members suggested to her that they offer me a job as a teacher. My mother didn't think it advisable but when they insisted, she said she would be a silent partner. I taught there four years. There were two families of colored children from there. The one family was new that year, having come from Arkansas to work for a vegetable gardner. There were four children. One was a boy of fifteen and in the second grade. He didn't cause me any trouble, but he simply couldn't learn. One Monday morning, the two men on the board came to the school and told me they were taking this boy out of school as they had learned that on Sunday in a fit of anger, he had killed their horse. They soon moved away.

My classes averaged from 5 to 8 grades and generally around 25 students. I taught Decker School south of Topeka for one year. Then I had a chance to teach Sunbeam School, the district north of my home. I taught there for two years. Later, I taught at Union School for 12 years, finishing my teaching career. One boy and one girl started and graduated with me.

My beginning salary was $75.00 and my highest was $105.00 per month. My first retirement check was $16.74 a month, and now I receive $173.56.

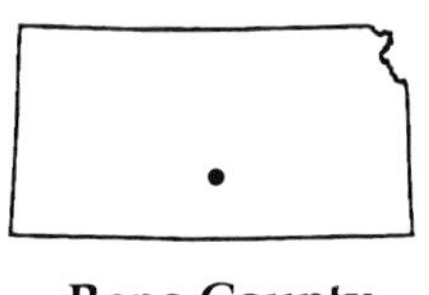

Reno County

Maintaining the Discipline

Adora (Tharp) Bryan

Topeka, Kansas

Mound School, District 34 - 1923-25

After graduating from the newly opened rural high school at Partridge, Kansas in Reno County, I knew it was time to think of making a living. College for me seemed out of the question. My parents could not afford it, and I had no inclination to work my way through, as those more ambitious were doing. A friend told me of a one-room school needing a teacher. It was only a few miles from where I attended school. The Mound School had gained a bad disciplinary reputation. The teacher, having never attended a one-room country school, was at a complete loss at the antics of the mischevious boys. They tormented her in many ways — pulling her dinner pail up the flag pole and being generally obnoxious. She gave up her job after they threw ink on her as she entered the room. She resigned near the end of her unfinished term. The board wanted a teacher who could bring calm and quiet to the schoolroom. Although I had no teaching experience, I convinced them that I could! I did and was rehired for the second year.

Early in my first year, at the board member's request, I asked the boys not to climb over the woven wire fence that surrounded the school yard. But "forbidden fruit" was too tempting, and one Friday evening, I observed these brothers climbing over to cut across the fields on their way home. They ran when they saw me. I did not pursue them, as the previous teacher was prone to do. I cogitated over the weekend, realizing it to be a volatile situation. Come Monday morning, the boys kept eyeing me and looking at each other. I said nothing. Recess came and went, but as I dismissed for the lunch hour, I requested the three boys return to see me. They came. It's impossible for me to repeat what was said, but I do remember I explained that a short memory must be remedied and the only way I knew to impress upon their minds was to punish them. The two smallest boys began to cry, but I paddled them and sent them out to play. The "big boy", twelve years old, was belligerent when I told him so stand. I took his arm and told him to bend over. He did and I administered the punishment with a strap I had for that purpose. It was the first and last time corporal punishment was administered.

The mouse story is an amusing one. Even though grades were separated by recitation periods, periods for writing and copy work was rather a quiet time for them all. I was busily occupied at my desk when a little tittering was heard. Looking up, I asked, "What's the matter?" One sweet faced little girl said, "Miss Tharp, there's a mouse under your desk"! Thinking it a ruse, I replied, "It will go away." I continued with my paperwork. At recess a little girl asked, "Aren't you afraid of mice?" I responded, "Oh, a mouse won't hurt you." She told me the previous teacher would climb upon her desk. No wonder she didn't complete her term. The kids tormented her to distraction. There were no more "mice."

Then there was Pete. He was not troublesome but had difficulty making his grades. He was lethargic, seemingly uninterested in school. I talked to him one day about his problems, and he was uncommunicative. I told him he was failing and would need to go back from third grade to second grade. He stubbornly shook his head, and his mouth tightened into a firm line. I explained how difficult it would be to go on when he hadn't near learned his multiplication tables or spelling words. He still sat, dejected. Then an inspiration came to me as I said, "Pete, do you think you could take both grades at once?" His face lit up and he looked at me with tears in his eyes as I told him we would try. I saw his mother and she asked me, "What have you done to Pete? He is a changed boy and can hardly wait to get to school." Indeed, he became a changed boy. In fact, he became an inspiration! His despair, and mine, had turned to hope.

Times change, we change, conditions change — yet without it there could be no progress. We learn, then put into practice the things that we find better suited to our needs. Always with our eyes on the needs of future generations.

My two years of teaching was a learning experience for me — one that served my many years I was married to a Kansas School Administrator. After his thirty years as an administrator, we moved to Topeka, and he served 20 years as Executive Secretary of the Kansas Teachers Retirement Board.

I am convinced that no amount of schooling can make a good teacher if she has not the innate ability to understand and love children, to inspire them to pursue their desires, to learn, and to incite their curiosity. God bless our teachers.

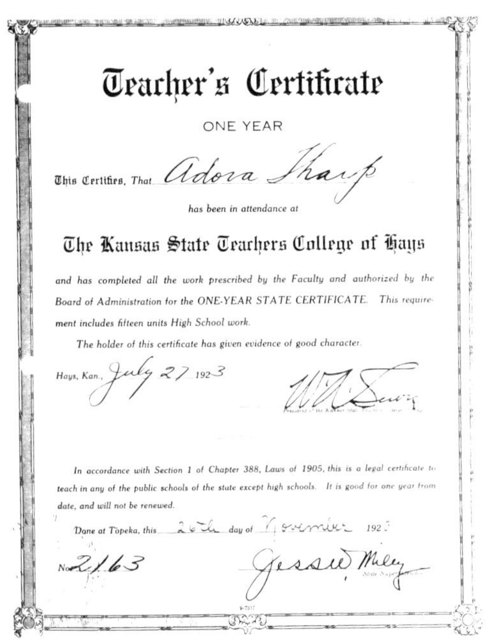

Teacher's Certificate

ONE YEAR

This Certifies, That Adora Tharp

has been in attendance at

The Kansas State Teachers College of Hays

and has completed all the work prescribed by the Faculty and authorized by the Board of Administration for the ONE-YEAR STATE CERTIFICATE. This requirement includes fifteen units High School work.

The holder of this certificate has given evidence of good character.

Hays, Kan., July 27 1923

In accordance with Section 1 of Chapter 388, Laws of 1905, this is a legal certificate to teach in any of the public schools of the state except high schools. It is good for one year from date, and will not be renewed.

Done at Topeka, this 26th day of November 1923

No. 2163

STATEMENT OF GRADES

FROM

COUNTY BOARD OF EXAMINERS,

OF

Reno County, Kansas.

Miss Adora Tharp
Partridge

The following is a statement of your grades in the examination held Jan 25-26 1924:

Spelling	84	Physiology and Hygiene,	83
Reading	70	Elements of Agriculture,	70
Writing	84	General Science	77
English Grammar and Composition	58	English Classics	81
Geography	63	Principles and Methods,	87
Arithmetic	77	Elements of Music	70
United States History	40	English History	
Kansas History	57	Elements of Physics	
Civil Government	63	Average standing	

REQUIREMENTS.

Third-grade certificates, minimum, 60 per cent; average, 75 per cent. Minimum age, eighteen years. No experience.

Second-grade certificates, minimum, 60 per cent; average, 80 per cent. Minimum age, eighteen years. Seven months' experience.

First-grade certificates, minimum, 75 per cent; average, 90 per cent. Minimum age, twenty years. Fourteen months' experience.

S. T. Howard, County Superintendent
Nellie Forrester, Associate Examiner
Stanley M. Tennant, Associate Examiner
County Board of Examiners.

FORM 32—C

No. 1

Teacher's County Certificate

Expires July 1 192

These Presents Declare, That M. Adora Sharp, having furnished satisfactory evidence of good moral character, and having passed the examination required by law, and being otherwise legally qualified to receive the same, is granted this

CERTIFICATE OF THE THIRD GRADE

which shall be valid in the Elementary Schools of Reno County for the term of One Year from the date hereof, unless revoked.

This Certificate can not be renewed without examination. It can not be indorsed in any other County of the State.

Given under our hands, at Hutchinson

County of Reno, State of Kansas,

this day of July 192

STANDING.

Required average, 75 per cent; minimum grade, 60 per cent.

Spelling.	84	Kansas History.	80
Reading.	78	Civil Government.	69
Writing.	89	Physiology and Hygiene.	73
English Grammar and Composition.	60	Elements of Agriculture.	65
Geography.	81	Elementary General Science.	73
Arithmetic.	60	English Classics.	80
United States History.	81	Principles and Methods of Teaching.	95

AVERAGE.

County Superintendent

Associate Examiner

Stanley M. Tennant, Associate Examiner

County Board of Examiners.

FORM 12 2-23-30,000

TEACHER'S CONTRACT

IT IS HEREBY AGREED, By and between School District No. 34, County of Reno, State of Kansas, and Adora M. , the holder of a certificate, this day in force, that said teacher is to teach, govern, and conduct the public schools of said district to the best of her ability, follow the course of study adopted by the State Board of Education, keep a register of the daily attendance and studies of each pupil belonging to the school, make all reports required by law, and such other reports as may be required by the County Superintendent and the State Superintendent of Public Instruction, and endeavor to preserve in good condition and order the schoolhouse, grounds, furniture, apparatus, and such other district property as may come under the immediate supervision of said teacher, for a term of eight school months, commencing on the third day of Sept, A. D. 1928, for the sum of eighty five dollars per school month, to be paid at the end of each school month.

It is also agreed that said teacher will pursue the professional course of study prescribed by the State Reading Circle Board, will attend county teachers' associations, and shall receive one dollar as compensation for each county teachers' association attended: *Provided*, That the District Clerk shall not draw an order in payment of compensation for such attendance of county teachers' meetings unless he shall have received written notice from the County Superintendent that said teacher is entitled to such pay.

It is also provided that in case said teacher shall be legally dismissed from school, or shall have her certificate legally annulled, by expiration or otherwise, then said teacher shall not be entitled to wages from and after such dismissal or annulment: *Provided further*, That the wages of said teacher for the last month of the school term shall not be paid until said teacher shall have made the reports hereinbefore mentioned.

And the said School District Board hereby agrees to keep the schoolhouse in good repair, pay for janitor service, and provide the necessary fuel, school register, and such other supplies as may be necessary.

IN WITNESS WHEREOF, We have hereunto subscribed our names, this 24th day of April, A. D. 1928

Clay Ziemar, *Director.*

ATTEST.

C. P. Martiney, *Clerk.*

Adora M., *Teacher.*

O. Schrock, *Treasurer.*

NOTE.—This contract should be made out in duplicate and one copy given to the teacher and the other preserved on file in the School District Clerk's office. The law does not authorize the School District Board to make a contract with a teacher nor to pay salary for any time during which a certificate is not in force.

Osborne County
Mitchell County

The Smell of New Clothes

Agnes Hennes

Interview by David Ottley and Gery Hake
Courtesy of Fort Hays State University

Osborne County — *Free Will School - 1925*
Mitchell County — *Hillside School Dist. 103 - 1926*
Fair View School - Dist. 144
Sunflower School

The first school I taught was Free Will School in Osborne county out in the prairie. Fact of the matter is, by running down in the pasture about a mile and a half or two, we'd find a stone that said geographic center of the United States.

All kids wore handmade clothes. No one thought of buying a ready-made dress; that was out. I remember I always enjoyed the first day of school because everyone was wearing a brand new dress or new overalls. I could smell that fabric all day long. It smelled like that until their clothes got washed. The girls, you never saw any bare skin. Their legs were covered.

I was at the blackboard writing out problems when a spitball hit me in the back. I turned around and said, "Frank, did you do that?"

"Yes."

"Well, why did you do that?"

"Because that other student bet me 15 cents I was afraid to do it." Little things like that happened and it made your day happy. I didn't take it as an insult, and no one else did either.

In that last school I taught I had all those students, I couldn't do justice. Time was just too short. I tried to do my best, but I know I failed them a little bit. Not that I wanted to, there just wasn't time. I had a couple of boys that were very disruptive. They talked a lot and were troublemakers. When you were teaching the rest of the classes they were problems. I think that is one thing that kind of burned me out about teaching. You had so many and then get a wild one - it doesn't work very well.

Antelope Ridge

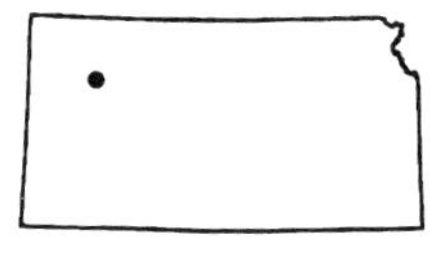

Gove County

Fred Crippen

from an interview by Walt Cooper
Courtesy of Fort Hays State University

Antelope Ridge, District 52 - 1924-25; Orion - 1925-26
East Lone Star - 1926-28; Spring Creek - 1928-29

I was just 17 years old when I went out to teach. I had just four boys. The school closed two weeks early because they moved to Quinter.

Your salary was written on your contract. They would say they would pay you so much, and if you decided you would take it, fine. The only say you would have was, "I'll take it."

They voted to organize Antelope Ridge in 1905 and the building was built in 1908. They sawed the rock, quarried the rock, and carried it up there and built the building. The unique part of the building was they planned off the inside of the rock, plastered it smoothly and used blackboard paint, and that was the blackboard. The roof was wood and it had to be hauled 20 or 30 miles from the railroad. It had a regular floor - 6" flooring is what they called it. It was a pine floor.

Antelope Ridge got its name because the people who lived there could see antelope running along the ridge.

The Antelope Ridge District #52 school was disorganized on May 24, 1936, twenty-eight years after it had opened.

Reasons for Teacher Turnover

Marion County

Ida Skibbe Wohlford

Geneseo, Kansas

Interview by Janet Porter, courtesy of Fort Hays State University

Finch School - 1925-27

After my sophomore year in high school, I decided to take normal training at Marion High School so I could teach.

The first year at Finch I received $75.00 a month. The second year, I got a raise and received $90.00.

I guess there was a problem with teacher turnover back in the 1920's. I guess marriage was one of the causes. If a teacher got married, in most cases her contract immediately ceased, and the school board would not hire a married teacher. Another reason for turnover was some teachers thought they would make a good teacher, but after one year they left the teaching profession. I guess another reason teachers left would be lack of discipline. If you couldn't keep the discipline and keep the school quiet, the children attending to their own business, there was no learning. Another reason for leaving the one-room school was to further education. That is what I did.

Most grades were promoted at the end of the year picnic. I gave each student a little book for a momento of their school year. When the 8th grade was completed, all the 8th graders in Marion County were included that passed their 8th grade exams. If the student received 90% or higher, he or she was given special recognition.

The day before the last day of school, the students and I would take our lunches and have a special picnic. Once we walked to some nearby rocks and caves, the children had fun exploring. We were tired by the time we got back to school. I guess you could call that a field trip.

Hodgeman County

Two Negro Families Made Up the School

Alice Weigel

by Jolene Rhine, courtesy of Fort Hays State University

One-room school near Jetmore - 1927-30

I taught country school right out of high school. That was all that was required for the country school. I applied to different schools and took the one I wanted because it was close to my home, and I could walk or ride horseback. I went to see Mrs. Pfiester, the head of the school board, and she asked questions about teaching. I told her I just got out of high school. She said, "These are colored children. Do you think you can handle that? I want them taught just like white children. That's important to me as a school board member." It didn't matter to me. There were two families, the Moore's and the Reed's. When I had been accepted, they sent me a notice.

I got to school on horseback the first year. The second year I bought a Model T Ford. Half the time I would get half way home and would have a flat or something. I had to walk the rest of the way and call the Paxton Garage to fix it. The tires were hard and women couldn't fix them. At the end of the school year, I didn't have a dime saved, it all went to the garage.

Schools were used for box suppers, pie suppers, but not so much in mine because of the small group I had. Two Negro families didn't do socializing like that. No social activity we could have had would make money for the school. There wouldn't have been a crowd.

Entertainment was Important

Mary Weisdorfer Yost

Cummings, Kansas

Atchison County

Float School District 27 - 1927-29; Fairground, District 4 - 1929-38
Clingan, District 68 - 1958-62; Shannon, District 25 - 1964

The governing body was a school board which consisted of a director, clerk and treasurer. They hired a teacher each spring for the next term, which was 8 months. There were politics involved of course, relatives entered in as well as friends. Qualification did not always make the decision. My first salary was $75.00 a month or $600.00 a year. One teacher taught for $25.00 per month as she stayed in her home, thus avoiding board and room. Salaries depended on the tax income from the specific district as there was no state aid. Another deciding factor was the number of students in the school. Not all districts were the same size or the same wealth to be taxed.

Another factor in selecting a teacher was her past record of programs she had produced. Three programs a year were expected and in most cases were for entertainment only as there were no VCRs or TVs and only a few radios. The first program was during the fall season and was for raising money. Refreshments were served following the program. The income was used to buy supplies for the school room or playground equipment. It was this program that played a part in getting a position for the next school term. Many districts changed teachers each year. It helped if one had a knowledge of music. Many didn't. The second program was Christmas and the third was the last day of school and this one was performed following an elaborate basket dinner at noon. Following the program, a period of anxiety ended when the report cards were distributed and immediately each pupil knew whether he had passed to the next grade. It was quite a scene to see the youngsters racing to their parents excitedly calling out, "I passed", and most of them did. This was a big affair and usually attended by all members of the community plus a few visitors.

A teacher was first a teacher plus the added titles of janitor, judge, counselor, nurse and playground activities director. The teacher was expected to be prepared to teach the following subjects: Grade 1-8, Reading and Literature, Arithmetic, English, U.S. and Kansas History, Physiology (Health now), Geography, Spelling, Agriculture and Writing. This involved a lot of classes and a teacher used different methods to try not to slight any. Sometimes the grades were combined, sometimes one could alternate classes, sometimes slip in an exam, thus some writing while others recited and upper grades could be doing independent studies.

Yes, we policed. We were always on the lookout for trouble. If it did show up, we had to have court session and there was no one else to judge. A teacher often played the mother role for various reasons such as sickness, home situations, loneliness, etc.

As a janitor, I would bring in water each morning (pump it) for drinking and for washing hands at noon. When it was cool or cold, I would bring in wood for the stove or as I did for many years, go down into an unfinished basement to start a furnace fire. There was coal in the basement. The school was by a railroad track and I was always afraid I would find a bum - I never did. After the floor was swept, I took home the daily papers to grade.

During the winter months, we had a hot lunch program. I would put a pan of water on the floor of the register or in my first school we used the top of the stove. The children would put their jars of cocoa or soup into the water. Sometimes it would be lukewarm and sometimes too hot to eat depending on the weather.

Once I had 40 students and only 39 desks. That year I had 6 beginners, 6 eighth graders and 3 seventh graders. It was most important to try to give the first graders a good start and it was important that the eighth graders pass their state examinations. It was important too, that the 7th graders were well prepared for the 8th grade. What we did for those intermediate grades, I don't know, but somehow they made it!

Fairground School

Shannon School

Eighth Grade Class
Pardee School, 1924
Atchison County

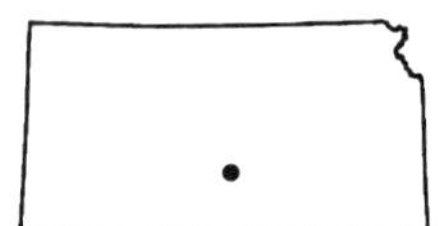

Teaching the Amish

Edith Lewis Young McKee

Reno County
1929-48

Olive School, Mt. Liberty School, Almstead School, North Reno (29 years)

I graduated from Castleton Rural High School in 1929. I went to the bank and borrowed $75.00 to pay tuition, board, and room at McPherson College in McPherson, Kansas. I attended a 6 week review course and at the end of the 6 weeks we went to the McPherson Courthouse where we wrote on 17 subjects in two days.

In 1929, there were many teachers trying to secure a job. I felt very fortunate in having a position. My first school had all 8 grades with four English speaking families and the rest were Amish. One first grade Amish girl could speak English and was my interpreter. There were eight first graders including a set of twin boys, Henry and Harvey Miller.

The Depression hit everyone hard except the Amish who always helped each other in any crisis. It didn't seem such a tragic time for them. My salary in 1929 was $80.00 per month. I stayed with the Clarence Haynes family for two years as they lived close to the school. When Clarence came after his daughter, Margaret, to take her home for lunch, he brought me a roaster full of delicious food. His wife, Letta, was a very good cook. When he brought Margaret back, he picked up the roaster.

In my third year of teaching, one of the girls could not start school as she had the mumps. She came back to school for a month and then was stricken with polio. She lost that year. The next fall I started working with her taking her through two years in one so she would be ready for the state exams for graduation. She passed them, too. During that year I carried her at least twice a day to the outdoor bathroom.

One morning during my 8 years at Almstead School, I began hearing the droning sound of airplanes. This was somewhere between 1940-45. I invited the children to come with me and we sat on the south steps of our building and watched a squadron of planes traveling northwest to southeast. As it was during the war, we never learned where they were from or where they were going.

One day around 3:30 or 4:00 p.m. when it was time to send the children home, I could see heavy clouds forming and I asked the children to come back in with me. This meant it was time to go to the basement steps. I told them to look to the southwest where there was a tornado on the ground. They saw it lift and go over us. In about thirty minutes I was able to give the all clear and the children went on their way home.

In May of 1990, I was invited to a reunion of the Olive School District. It had to be held in another school as the Olive building had been converted to a home in Haven, Kansas, many years ago. In the school yard, were horses and buggies, modern cars and vans. The afternoon was spent reminiscing over golden school days of the past. One member of the 1929 school board was Dale Shapin. He was 94 years old and gave many interesting insights of the school. Another original board member, Julius Pop, 96 years old, attended and told us many interesting things. Three of the old order Amish girls sang songs that I had taught them so many years ago. We talked about the games we played like Fox and Geese, Last Couple Out, Drop the Handkerchief, Baseball and Musical Chairs. My forty-seven years in the public schools were very challenging and rewarding.

Osage County

Box Suppers, Programs and Games

Fannie Alling
Topeka, Kansas

District 3, Junction, Bailey, Wilson, West Tequa and Michigan Valley

I began teaching in the fall of 1927 after graduating from Lyndon High School, Osage County, Kansas. I taught four years then married, four years later started teaching again and taught 8 years.

All one-room schools had windows on each side, a furnace type coal stove in the center of the room. This was the best kind of heating at that time. The teacher did all the janitor work, built fires each cold morning, carried out the ashes. Ashes made a good walk to the outside toilet - a toilet for boys and a toilet for girls. The teacher had to keep these clean and see paper was furnished which was a Montgomery Ward or Sears catalog. The coal bins were usually built away from the schoolhouse. One school had the coal bin attached, that was great! Kerosene lamps in brackets on the window casings lighted the buildings for evening gatherings. To start the fires in the stoves, paper and cobs were used. Kerosene was also used and one had to be careful with this as it might cause an explosion. Each school had a small room in front to hang coats and place overshoes. The water bucket was there with the wash pan. A dipper was in the bucket to drink from until each child brought their own cup. Later, earthen containers with a spigot were used. Water was pumped from a well or cistern on the school grounds.

The school board consisting of usually three men hired the teacher and made the rules. Prayer, Bible reading and flag salute were held every morning and singing was desired. I was asked to be on the school ground during the noon hour and the two 15 minute recesses. Box suppers in the fall were for entertainment and a program by the children was required. Then the decorated boxes containing delicious food were auctioned and the highest bidder got the box. The money was used to buy things for the school. A Christmas program was also required. The teacher gave each child a sack of candy and sometimes a small gift. On the last day of school there was a program and a big dinner. School doors were removed and placed across the desks and used for tables on which to place the food. Each family brought their own table service.

Games played at noon and recess were Baseball, Anti-over, Tag, London Bridge and during the winter, Fox and Geese. The boys would build snow forts and have a war with snow balls. Inside the school they played Musical Chairs, Hide the Thimble, and Tit-Tat-Toe.

Each child carried their own lunch. In winter, a pan with water would be placed on the stove and a container would be set in the pan so the children could have something brought from home heated.

All eight grades were taught, sometimes only one child in a grade. One school there were 24 pupils and all eight grades.

The United States flag was hoisted each morning, weather permitting, and brought in after school hours.

The teacher's salary was low, $50.00 per month for eight months - $70.00 was the highest wage. The teacher had to stay in the district and pay for room and board out of the low wage. Usually the teacher had a nice place to stay.

Homesick for Osawatomie

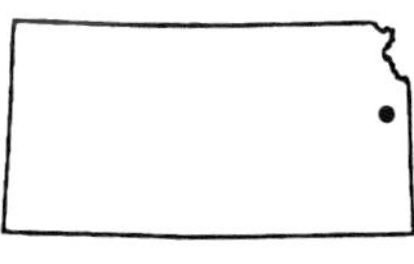

Miami County

Bess LaMatry
Columbia, Missouri

Union School, Elm Grove School, Crescent Hill School, Plum Creek School, Rose Valley School, Stockwell School

In the year 1927 after graduating from high school in Kansas I was ready to take the State Examination to get a certificate to teach school. This over and having passed the exam getting the State Teaching

Certificate, my next step was to find a teaching position.

For this I went to the County Seat of Miami County to the County Superintendent's office. She was in charge of all districts and knew the rural schools which needed teachers. After having done this I was provided with the name of the school, location in the county, and the names of three school board members of that rural school.

This school was sixteen miles from my home, and in the days before paved roads, this was quite far from home. My mother, a friend and I set out to find the first of the three school board members. The man was over in a field at least a quarter of a mile from the road, riding a harrow, kicking up the dirt and dust. As I had sprained an ankle the day before this, I crutched through the plowed ground to where the farmer was working. That done, and after talking to him, I was given direction to the houses of the other two board members. They hired me to teach their school. The salary was eighty dollars a month. I was told by one of the board members I could board and room just across from the school. The end of the first month I learned I had another trek to each school board member's house. From one member I got a thing called a voucher. I took the voucher to another member, and he wrote the check.

A word about the home where I spent the next eight months. They were good people. They tried to be good to me, insisting I should drink a cup of hot coffee before starting out each morning to teach. I didn't care for coffee, and this only annoyed me. Also, they would correct me each time I called them Mr. or Mrs. Johnson, as the case might be. Mrs. Johnson would say, "My name is Leona", and Mr. Johnson would say, "My name is Wilbur." I had been taught by my mother to say Mr. and Mrs. so I never learned that either. The Johnsons would be right on the mark today, being so informal.

Homesickness really set in during the time I was not at school. I thought, "Dear Lord, I shall surely die tonight." This was the first time I had ever spent a night away from my home. My parents came after me on the weekends, During this year, the deep ruts in the roads wore out my father's Essex car.

At school I enjoyed teaching all eight grades. There were at least eight first grade children for me to teach beginning reading. Somehow they learned very well and as I recall the secret of it all that year was repetition. I used word lists, and we would go over them every day.

I was only seventeen years old, and the world at school was mine. We were to be supervised by the County Superintendent. She was to visit us at any time in the year. She never came. I guess the roads were too rutty.

Today schools have to put up with censorship of books. I was the censor of the books here. I proceeded to think the book, ***The Pit and the Pendulum,*** by Edgar Allen Poe was unfit for young minds to read. Instead of taking it off a list, I just went to the stove, the old Smith Heating System that burned coal,, and pitched it in the flames, and it was gone. Needless to say, next morning, three board members (men) were there to greet me. Their wrath was fury, but I was undaunted — I talked right back to them.

Also, I recall that a little first grade boy fell down on the playground and complained of his shoulder. I examined it. There was only a tiny red spot, but by the time school was over for the day his little shoulder was hanging down. Of course, this was a black spot against me, as the parents took the child to a doctor and found the shoulder collar bone was broken.

Needless to say, I never wanted to teach there again, as school ended, nor did I think I wanted to go away from home to teach anywhere ever again.

By August of that year, I had recovered somewhat from that experience of the first year. In late August an older and much wiser school teacher than me came by to visit and suggested I go apply for the only school left in the country without a teacher. She advised it was not too great to sit around and be poorer with no income at all, however little it might be. She took me, though I was a bit reluctant to apply, and get a contract for that school, which was fully as far from home as I as the first year. Again I boarded across the road from the schoolhouse. I was still homesick but maybe a tad better than the year before.

This school was close to a Missouri Pacific train route, from Kansas City south. One rainy, rainy Friday evening, no one was there to take me away home for the weekend. I called my home, and my mother told me that the rivers, both the Marais Des Cygnes River and the Pottawatomie were out of their banks and there was no way in or out of town except by the good old Missouri Pacific trains. After hanging up the telephone, I called the nearest station stop and was told a fast passenger train would be going through there soon. I asked if it stopped there. He said, "No, only if you flag it." I told the man of the house, "We can flag the train." He got his lantern, raincoat, boots, umbrellas and we set out to the railroad track to get the train that would take me home for the weekend. When we saw the train coming down the track, he got in the middle of the track and frantically waved his lantern and the train came to a dead stop. Two uniformed men stepped off the train, the conductor and the brakeman. They said, "What's the matter lady, is there a cow on the tracks?" At this I rushed past them getting quickly on the train and uttering as I went, "Nothing is wrong. I'm just going to Osawatomie." They followed me back to the seat where I sat down. They looked at me and then to one another. One said, "Osawatomie did you say?" I said, "Certainly, to Osawatomie." Then they again looked knowingly at each other — Osawatomie. Well, since that was the town noted for the Insane Hospital in the state, they thought it best to leave me be. I, feeling I had done nothing improper, rode safely home to Osawatomie. My father was a railroad employee and the story went through his circle of friends, much to my father's embarrassment, I am certain.

The third year I succeeded in being hired by a school board close to home. This school was four miles out in the country. My father bought a horse for me to ride. This horse, named Ole Buck, lived up to his name. I would ride him to the end of the pavement, where he would buck and buck until I would get off crying, tie him up and hitch a ride behind a friend who came by on her big draft horse. I rode with her as far as she had to go to her school, then got off and walked the remainder of the way. In cold weather, the fire had to be started to make the room warm by the time the children arrived.

I went on to teach a total of ten years in rural schools. Eight of those years I lived at home.

Restored and Remembered

Marguerite Erickson Buffon
Emporia, Kansas

Lower Fox Creek School - 1929-30

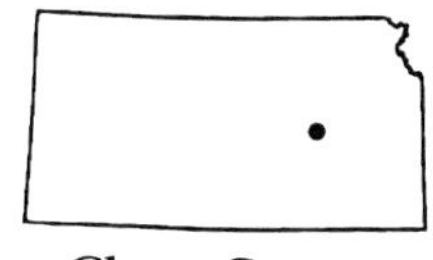

Chase County

This is the story of the Lower Fox Creek School in Chase County, the way I remember. . .

I, Marguerite (Erickson) Buffon was ready for the third grade when my folks moved to the Lower Fox Creek School District. This school is located about three miles north of Strong City, Kansas. North of this school another three or four miles was Upper Fox Creek School. They were both located near the Fox Creek. Each district was made up of four or five families and everyone walked to school. We lived a mile from school.

Lower Fox Creek School is a stone school house facing east and located on a hill. Windows were on the south and north. There were black boards in back and between the windows. A big pot bellied stove stood toward the back. There was a small stage in front of the schoolhouse for the teacher's desk and to be used for school programs. There were book shelves and also shelves for lunch buckets. There was a cistern at the northeast corner of the schoolhouse. Each student had his or her own cup. We washed our hands in a pan, but I can't remember about towels. We had individual seats and a recitation bench.

We had very good teachers and a full curriculum. We went eight months a year. The teachers stayed in the neighborhood. They always stayed at my folks' home and they had to walk to school just like we did.

As the years went by, new things were tried. Hot lunches were a new thing. We had cocoa and different kinds of soup to supplement our cold lunches. The soup was cooked on top of the coal stove all morning. Ingredients for the soup were sent by the parents. We each had our own soup bowl.

Instead of community meetings, we had soup suppers ever so often. We were taught how to eat and pass food correctly. We also had neighborhood hayrack rides for entertainment.

We played games like Darebase, Blackman, Anti-over, Baseball,

Hide and Seek, and Tag. We read stories out of the Mother West Wind Books, Why stories, Where stories and When stories. We usually had a Christmas program and something in the spring before school was out. The last day of school we would have a big dinner or a picnic.

One highlight of the year was when the County Superintendent visited our school. We took eighth grade exams sent out by the Superintendent to be able to go to high school.

My school days at Lower Fox Creek were from about 1917 to 1923. I then went to the Chase County Community High School and graduated in 1928. I had started to school when I was five so I was quite young when I graduated. I took a Post Graduate year and then with a Normal Training Certificate taught at Lower Fox Creek School in 1929-1930. I got $50.00 a month and had four students. One of the students was my little sister, Bernice. At the end of that year the school was closed for lack of pupils.

When I taught, the coal stove was replaced by natural gas and a piano and many more books were added.

The Lower Fox Creek School still stands and a Garden Club cares for it as one of their projects. One thing that is different is the road. It is now located up the hill in front of the schoolhouse. It used to be down the hill to the east, the highway made the change.

Sometime during my school years a fire destroyed the inside of the building. We went to school in a vacant house while it was being repaired. I forgot to say that the schoolhouse has a belfry with a big bell. There were two outside toilets and in back of the schoolhouse there was a coal shed. These are gone except for one toilet. The play yard was big and down the hill to the south.

I haven't been over to the school for sometime, but old things are being brought in from other old schools and it has been restored to make it a wonderful schoolhouse again.

Lower Fox Creek School
Students consisted of three families
The Ericksons, Atkins and Bruces
(I am left on the front row)

Lower Fox Creek School After Fire
No Belfry Yet

Chapter Two

Memories of the teachers during the 1930's and 40's reflect the hard times. Alenna Sanders of Nortonville writes that in the 1930's teachers were "a dime a dozen." The Great Depression, dust storms, and droughts marked this era as the "dirty thirties." It was a time of "make do, do it yourself, or do without", and the one-room schoolteachers of Kansas met the challenge. Ella Aley of Topeka writes of "depression" suppers at her school. "Everybody came, everybody ate, and nobody paid."

Feed sack dresses, flour sack underwear, and brown oxford shoes were the fashion for the girls of the Kansas one-room schools during this time. Many parents made the girls wear long brown stockings that bagged at the knees and showed the wrinkles and folds of long underwear. No girl remembers this as a pleasant experience! Sometimes slacks were worn under dresses during the cold walk to school, but had to be removed upon arrival. The boys wore uniforms of bib overalls with flannel or blue chambray long sleeved shirts. Sometimes their shirts were "mama made" from feed sacks. They wore leather high top, lace up work shoes. They were dressed just as their fathers - miniature farmers.

Change came about in the 1940's with World War II. Kansas teachers again met the challenge of rationing, family separation, and participation in the war effort. Newspaper and scrap drives were one way of "doing your part." Teachers would take students out to the fields to gather milkweed pods for use in making lifesaving vests.

Many teachers and community members left for better paying jobs in defense plants and other war related industries. Now teachers were not so plentiful, and salaries climbed a little higher. Patriotism was stressed in the schools, and students were taught the songs of the Armed Forces. Children could be heard singing "Anchors Aweigh" and the "Marine's Hymn" as they walked down the dirt roads toward the clanging 8:30 a.m. bell. Teachers would allow students to run outside to view the droning U.S. war planes overhead. This was an exciting scene for the farm children of Kansas.

Rural schools were being wired for electricity at this time as the REA poles began dotting the rural countryside. Electricity greatly improved the lighting situation inside the school building. Few schools had restrooms or indoor plumbing. Teachers asked for telephones to be installed, not as a luxury, but as a necessity. They met emergencies alone, relying on their own knowledge and common sense.

Neighbors helped neighbors get by - that's the way it was for Kansas farm folk. The school was the center of the community, and the monthly meetings lended support and encouragement to all. It didn't matter if the farmers had children attending the school. They went to the meetings as a part of the community.

Teaching in the '30's

Atchison County
Washington

Alenna Hawk Sanders
Nortonville, Kansas

Teachers were a dime a dozen. They had 20 teachers for every position. Married teachers were unheard of. The lowest salary in Atchison County was $35.00 per month and the highest was $60.00 per month for an 8 month term. Everyone's salary was published. Teachers were everything from principal to custodian —special ed teacher, P.E. teacher, music teacher, librarian and sometimes the babysitter

Aides for teachers were not necessary. Upper grade students helped the other children. Parent-teacher conferences were not necessary because parents and teachers met every month at the community meeting. Problems were discussed at this time. Room mothers were unheard of. Teachers sponsored and paid for their own parties. The usual supplies that were provided at the beginning of the year were one box of chalk and a package of construction paper. If the teacher asked for more,

Alenna Hawk Sanders

Washington School
Atchison County

they were considered wasteful. No degree was necessary to be an elementary teacher if you took Normal Training and passed the county examination.

If a young lady teacher had a boyfriend, he must never call on her during the middle of the week. This might keep her from doing a good job. Maybe this is where the saying "Old Maid School Teacher" came from.

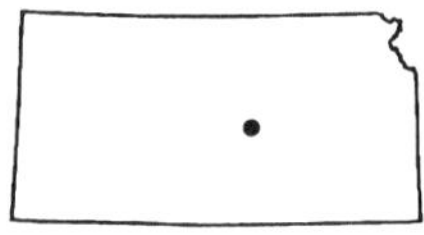

McPherson County

Teaching the Swedish and the German

Lois Ely Johnston

from an interview by Herbert D. Zook

Courtesy of Fort Hays State University

Prairie Queen #110, 1930-35
Clark School, NW of Inman

In my first school they were all Swedish people and were Lutheran or Lutheran types. The second school I taught was Holderman (Mennonite) and German.

In the Swedish school we had PTA once a month. The school would be packed every time. They would have supper or maybe just desserts. But such food you wouldn't believe! Everybody turned out. There were two old bachelors in their 50's. They wouldn't miss it. They were the first ones there with the lanterns and to light the lanterns for me. Then we'd have Christmas programs and programs on the last day. We'd go all out to decorate. I don't know how we did it. They'd bring in a Christmas tree almost to the ceiling of the building and we put lighted candles on this thing. I shudder to this day with the building packed, and I remember the kids wanted to decorate the ceiling like it was snowing. They ran threads all around and pasted on balls of cotton and it looked just like it was snowing. The back of the stage was decorated with sheets tacked up. It was all homemade.

In the German school I had a problem. They wanted to speak their language which I didn't understand, and I guess it was close enough to one of the wars that we were not to speak the German language. I tried to keep them from doing this, and it became quite a problem. This was more on the school ground during recess and noon. I felt sometimes they were not saying good things.

When I was at the German school there was a little boy that lived 2 miles from school. I had no telephone. I had my car there, and he had an accident in his clothes that day. There was just no way he could stay there. What was I to do? He was in such bad shape, so I just put papers on the seat and left school in charge of a big boy I could trust and took this boy home — 2 miles. I reported to the school board and said I must have a telephone, and so they put one in. That was an improvement.

Graduation from both of these schools was held at the McPherson May Day. Even when I graduated the graduates walked in the parade — that's the way they graduated at McPherson.

At the last school I had a bunch of boys and they were kind of bad. I said "If you boys all pass I'll take you for an airplane ride on May Day." They all passed, and we went up in an open plane and it began to miss up there. I didn't think about being responsible for kids getting killed. It didn't sound too good to me, but we made it back down.

These Holderman boys were big boys and one morning before school I heard a commotion out on the playground. There were 17 boys in the outhouse raising cane and kicking the sides out. I said to myself "What do I do?" So I said, "You boys come out of there!" and they didn't. So I said, "If you don't come out of there, I'm coming in!" The biggest one came out first. They walked just like Indians into the classroom and sat down in their seats.

The things I remember mostly are pleasant and I enjoyed both schools of those early years very much. I loved the people at each place for what they were and what they tried to become while I was there.

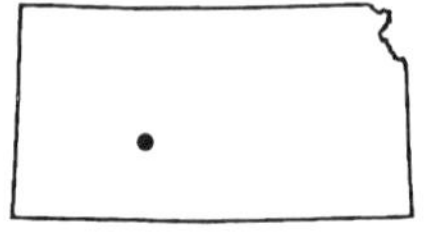

Pawnee County

Cooked Possom was not Appreciated

Ruth Johnson Shumate
Beloit, Kansas

Couchman School, 1932; Freeport School, 1938

I graduated from high school in 1930. Times were truly hard and I laid out of school one year. In the fall of 1931, I started college at Ft. Hays working for a three year state certificate. On completion of that year I was hired to a one-room school - grades 1-8. I know I had 2 eighth graders and two first graders and enough more in between to make 12 students.

I was young and learned much by the time I was through.

I built my own fires in a huge corner stove, carried coal and ashes, swept the floors, washed blackboards and heated water on the stove for the kids to wash hands before noon. We all drank from a carried in bucket of water pumped from a hand pump. Toilets were outdoor 2 holers and it was my job to keep them clean.

These were "Dust Day" years and more than once three school board members would come in on Monday with a broom and scoop shovels to help clean and carry out the dirt that had blown in over the weekend.

We had a sand table in which we did projects — maybe a Japanese village, complete with pagodas and small bridges. We also had crafts and made wood corner shelves, bread boards, and other things with all hand power.

We gave school programs and I played the piano which was an advantage.

The kids rode horses to school, and one family had four boys and one horse!

One family of two boys walked a mile across the field and had a string of traps which they tended. One instance still haunts me — they had caught a 'possum and the next day or so presented me with a delectable morsel of cooked 'possum. They loved it but I passed saying that I would enjoy it for supper. They also brought me a hog snake which they had caught — just a little fellow he was — but I can not tolerate to this day a small or large snake. But that day, I took it gingerly in two fingers and held it for their benefit.

In later years I married an uncle of four of my pupils. Uncle Robert was quoted often but at the time I had no interest.

After three years at Couchman School — named after early settlers — I moved to Freeport where I had 5 kids, 4 beginners and 1 seventh grader. Truly a schooling for motherhood! They were fun. One little guy was extra bright and a tag-along in his family. He was upset with me when I married at midterm, saying he planned to marry me when he grew up. The seventh grade girl was a joy to me — a friend and helper with the little ones. Believe it or not, we did a short Christmas program with those five little kids.

We had an old wood burning stove in the middle of the room and had Coleman lamps for lights at this school. Sometimes I wonder how I did it. I had to be innovative to accomplish what we did. I was fortunate to be able to drive from my parents home to both schools.

I have lost track of many students, and it is hard for me to realize that some of them are old people — 64 years old. I am 80 and cherish most every event that transpired.

P.S. We had a dog that regularly came to school with those four kids.

Fourteen Memories

Fausta J. Nicodemus

St. Francis, Kansas

Decatur County

Lyle School, 1927-29; Decatur School, 1930-32; Vallonia School; Logan School, 1933-34; North Valley School, 1935-37; Beaver Valley School, 1938-40

Unlike present day teachers who apply many places for employment, I never did apply for a school. I always was approached by board members.

1. Was highest paid rural teacher. Taught 14-28 pupils all grades.

2. Taught art, music, drama, had box suppers and programs.

3. Originated the first rural "zone" track meet. Planning events for parents, too. Women drove cars between nail kegs placed in croquet formation. The winner didn't knock over a keg.

4. Had ciphering and spelling matches as well as geography matches.

5. Friday afternoon oral reading with pupils choosing the subject.

6. Playing on the school ground with pupils — later caused me to have knee replacement. I jumped to prevent my stepping on a first grader as he fell in front of me while playing "Blackman". He raised up just as I jumped, causing me to fall on my knees into a pile of packed ashes.

7. I always placed desks facing the north and hung maps on the north wall to create a correct feel of location on maps.

8. A little frightened first grade girl kicked me in the stomach when I tried to console her, leaving the shoe sole print on my white dress all day.

9. Finding used cob pipes in windows and tobacco spit in the coal pail. It had such an odor that I refused to hold school until the board cleaned the mess and aired the building.

10. Holding on to a man's coat tail to find my way home to my boarding place when a black dust storm arrived at 4:30 p.m.

11. Finding "smooth" snake tracks in dust on my desk.

12. Singing a solo "Be the Best of Whatever You Are" at County Eighth Grade Commencement.

13. I did not favor consolidation of schools as I thought if the teacher was qualified in art, music, drama, etc., it was much better to keep rural schools open. Too many hours on school buses and lack of personal contacts for needed help and attention were concerns of mine.

14. A motto each month, on the front blackboard served to interest and I hope challenge the older pupils, such as "Character is what you are but reputation is what people think you are."

I thoroughly enjoyed my teaching experiences and appreciate contacts with former pupils such as the reunion at Sappa State Park in 1978 and the alumni banquet.

Hard Times

Veneita Lawrence Newton
Whiting, Kansas

Atchison County

Rose Hill; Muscotah Grade School

My first hitch at teaching was in 1928 to 1933. Wages ranged from $55.00 to $90.00 per month. I built fires, carried in drinking water, scrubbed outhouses, traveled on mud roads, prepared programs, had box suppers - no teacher's aides. Serious study in schooltime and fun and games at recess. We rang an 8:30 a.m. bell and all lessons were planned by the teacher, also grades recorded - no help.

My first husband died of a heart attack and I was never going to teach again. There were two little boys, and a little girl on the way, after all I had no time to pine. When the boys were in high school and the girl in the eighth grade, there was an opening and need for teachers, this was about 1950. Also a need for money as college came nearer. This also meant I had to go to night and summer school. My first schools were

Certificate of Award

This is to Certify that

Of School District No. 41 Jackson County, Kansas

is recommended for

Punctual and Regular Attendance

having been neither absent nor tardy for a period of five months.

Given at Holton Kansas this ___ day of ___ 19__

Teacher

County Superintendent

taught out of high school with only a test at age 18. By now I had remarried and we still lived on a farm. An offer of $1200 per year of 8 months looked much better than a little less than $500.00 per year. I taught 13 years in a one-room country school grades 1-8, and 9 years in Muscotah. grades 5 and 6. In the country school you were principal, judge, manager, in charge of music programs. Every student took part, not just the better student.

Oh yes, we cleaned up after sick children and did not have phones in the school.

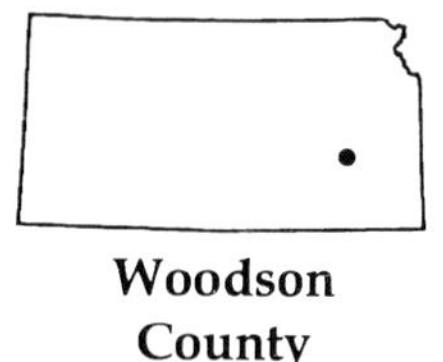

Woodson County

No Time for Pie Suppers or Programs

Orville Eugene Etter

from a taped interview by Jolene Rhine

Courtesy of Fort Hays State University

Finney School, Dist. #49, 1930-32
West Buffalo, Dist. #28, 1934

I took a normal training course in high school and started teaching immediately after I graduated. I rode horseback 4 1/2 miles each way. One night I left the schoolhouse, and it was beginning to rain. By the time I got home 3 1/2 inches had fallen. It rained hard. When I got on top of the hill, the horse turned tail to the wind and wouldn't go. Thunder rolling, lightening flashing - they say that's an awful dangerous place to be for lightening, but I got through it.

Sometimes schools did have evening programs but I didn't. I didn't have time to work with the youngsters to put on that. I felt it was more beneficial to them to give time to their own studies, rather than put on a program for the entertainment of the parents, and that was usually all an evening program was for. . . the women or young ladies of the district would bring pies and sell them, and use that money to buy athletic equipment. We didn't need that, so I didn't see any point in staging a pie supper.

There was one boy whom I had — I could work with him and work with him, and he could not remember how to spell cat from one evening to the next morning. Some 50 years later he was sheriff of a county and led the process of recovering a body from Lake John Redman Reservoir. So it makes you wonder about how effective your schoolwork has been.

In 1937, I finished my degree and went to Medicine Lodge and taught in high school. I taught there 4 1/2 years and then after I had my Master's and the war broke out, I went to the factory to work as an engineer. After commercial planes were designed and ready for production, I knew I'd be laid off so I got this job here in Hays (at the Math Department at Ft. Hays University). I didn't stay with it very long, just 34 years.

Caught in a Blizzard

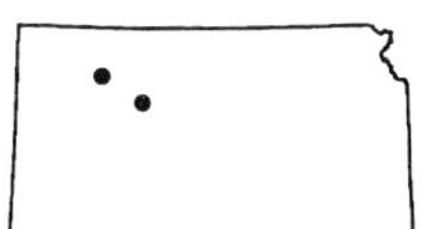

Ellis County
Sheridan County

Mary Traun

from a taped interview by Marie Burns
Courtesy of Fort Hays State University

South Walker, Hope Valley, District #6
Phillips School - Sheridan Co.

I got caught in a terrible blizzard with 6 children in my car, and to get to the place where I boarded we had to drive almost a half a mile through a field. There was a road through the field. I thought I could follow by way of the posts, but there were no posts here and everything was snow. I found myself going in circles and wound up in the corner of a section. I recognized the corner of the section by the mailboxes so I left my car. By then it was stranded. . . just no way could I find my way. I had a blanket in the car and I had the children all grasp a hold of that and I led. We walked a quarter of a mile down the hill to another farm house. By then their little fingers were frostbitten, some of them. My knees were frostbitten. I had boots on luckily. The lady got some snow and thawed us out and kept us all night. Now, that did turn me against western Kansas, I'll be honest with you.

The first year I taught at Phillips School there were 2 pupils, a sister and brother. The little fellow was just beginning. He couldn't speak a word of English. His sister was a 7th grader. It was a large school and there were just two children and rather than heat the big room with coal, I moved the two benches in the small library room. This was the only room we heated, and saved money for the district. Times were hard. The depression had set in back in 1932. Word got around and so I jumped from 2 students to 11 the next year.

At one time Hope Valley just took care of the English. The Catholic families, the Volga Germans, the High Germans, and the Low Germans did not send their children to these public schools. Well, they became more economical, started visiting with each other and decided to send them to public schools, the heck with driving those 7 miles a day. So they rebuilt and moved it out of the valley. Hope Valley is the name of the school yet and was until they closed it and moved it a mile and a half north, then it was torn down.

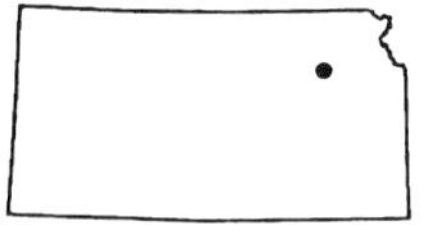

Shawnee County

Victor School Restored

Bennie Jr. Martinek
Rossville, Kansas

Victor School, District 101 - 1931-38

Victor School

The number of pupils varied from 5 to 27 and from three grades to all eight grades.

My term of teaching included the worst of the great depression and dust storms.

Victor School, District 101 is now located in the Ward Meade Park, Topeka.

County Nurse Helps

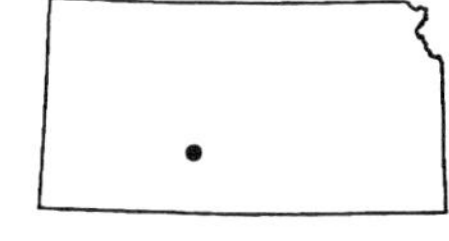

Edwards County

Loraine Ary
Greensburg, Kansas

Breitenbach School, 3 miles south of Belpre, Kansas
1932

The Capitol building in Topeka, Kansas is a very interesting place to visit. There is a series of large oil paintings on the walls of the rotunda of the large central lobby. The history of the state is told in these paintings. It is a history of courage, hope, frustrations and untold hardships to make dreams a reality. These paintings were not all finished as the artist was dismissed because the legislators were not happy with all the pictures. A Mr. Winter was commissioned to finish them. One of the pictures he painted depicted a one room country school. He had once lived in Belpre, Kansas, in Edwards County, and had personally known a little one room school known as the Breitenbach School because it was located on the Roy Breitenbach land three miles south of Belpre. In the picture a school teacher was urging the pupils to hurry to a storm cellar when a tornado threatens in the background.

This painting held special significance for me as this was the school where I taught my first year of school.

It was 1932. I was a sophomore at Kansas State College in Manhattan. I was taking a course in Home Economics. My father had been a successful farmer and he and my mother, a retired school teacher, had always had a deep interest in education. That year crops had been bad, the country was in a deep recession and wheat dropped to 25 cents a bushel. There was not money enough for me to go on to college. The second semester I changed my major to Elementary Education, did my practice teaching and earned my 60 hour certificate. This became a Life Certificate after I taught three years.

About 3½ miles from my home was this Breitenbach school. The year before, the school building had burned down the night before school started. No one knew how the fire started as the building had no electricity. The young man teacher was paid his years salary to fulfill their contract with him.

The school board decided to rebuild the building. This was a surprising development since it was only three miles from the Belpre city school and there were only the children from two families attending.

One family had a large family of boys and lived in a two room house. One board member commented that the parents treated their hogs better than they treated their children.

Another family had about 9 children. This family was clean, even when it meant washing clothes after the children had gone to bed, as there were not extra changes of clothing. This family had one child in each of the first seven grades. Their only means of transportation was horseback or a horse and wagon. About every two weeks or so the father drove an old stripped down Ford into Belpre for staples of groceries such as sugar, coffee and things they could not grow on their farm.

The boys in both families learned to trap and shoot wild animals for food and the small amount of money from the pelts. On several occasions I had to send a member home when he checked a trap on the way to school and was sprayed by a skunk.

I applied to the school board for the job of teaching this school. One of the board members, a farmer, told me that they had had an applicant who could not tell him how many pounds a bushel of ear corn weighed. I knew how much a bushel of wheat weighed, also a bushel of shelled corn, but not ear corn. We rather talked around the subject, so I never had to show my ignorance. I signed a contract for eight months at $75.00 a month.

I had 12 children in school that year. I was janitor, which meant cleaning the school house, seeing that we had a bucket of coal and kindling for the fire in the pot bellied heater in the back of the schoolroom. One morning I remember going to school when it was 18 degrees below zero, and building a fire. Several of the boys were larger than I was. I could usually get their help for the heavier jobs. Water had to be pumped by hand and carried into the school in a bucket. There was a single dipper everyone shared. There were two outhouses — one for boys and one for girls. Also a shed for the horses they rode to school. One end had a room for coal and kindling. To build a fire we soaked a few corn cobs in kerosene in a can. We laid them in first on the grates, then laid additional dry corn cobs or small sticks over these. When you struck a match they easily lighted and you were soon able to add several shovels of coal. Coal burned a long time and gave off very warm heat.

It was very hard to teach all the subjects in seven grades each day. Reading, writing, arithmetic, spelling were taught in all the grades with Kansas History, geography and Kansas agriculture added in the upper grades. Seventh and eighth grades had to go to the county seat to take the seventh and eighth grade exams to complete credentials to enter high school.

One of the Smith boys was my only 7th grader. I took him to Kinsley to take three exams. He was more fearful of going the 18 miles to a strange town in a strange building, than of the test itself. He had only been through Kinsley once in his life at night time as they moved to their farm at Belpre. He really did well and passed the test.

Each county had a County Superintendent and a County Nurse. They visited each school in the county regularly. The County Nurse was visiting our school and one boy had a very offensive odor. The nurse had him take off his dirty socks and heavy work shoes. There she found that he had huge sores on his foot. One toe had only the bone left. He had never complained about it hurting. The nurse went after the mother and showed her how to soak the foot in an antiseptic solution and gave her some ointment to put on it. She was to do this once a day. He was to put on clean socks each time. As the mother left she turned to the nurse and told her, "I hain't promising you nothing." The boy did get better and I certainly appreciated the nurse's help.

Sometimes when there were not enough hours in the day to get around to everyone, I would let an older child listen to the younger ones read or help with other studies. This kept the quicker children occupied and gave special tutoring to the slow ones. So much was learned in the one room schools from the other children reciting. They would listen as the older children read and discussed history or stories from our "Classic" books. They seemed very real.

Most country schools had 15 to 20 students. However, there were as many as 40 in some schools. This was too many students for one teacher and they probably did not get a very good education. I went through eight grades in a one-room country school. It was about 4 miles from the Breitenbach School. It was District 23. We had a Superior

School and our teacher had to have 3 years experience and a Life Certificate. We had a good library, and a music teacher came out once each week from Lewis for our music instruction. We usually had 14 to 18 students. This school gave their pupils a good education.

Until about 1910, there were no high schools in this area. My father went through eight grades and then went to Business School at Salina and graduated. My mother was living in Kirksville, Missouri and finished grade school. Then she entered the Missouri State Normal School where she got her degree and teaching certificate. Her brother was on the school board at Belpre. They needed a teacher, so she came to Belpre and taught. That is how my father and mother met.

The school was the center for entertainment in most areas. The last day of school was always looked forward to because the patrons brought in well filled baskets of food for a bountiful meal. Planks were placed over the desks for long tables. The children sat at one table and the men at the other one. The women waited on the tables.

During the winter "Literaries" were held between schools. One month one district would be host to another school. Then it was reversed. The teacher prepared some numbers with the children. Other numbers were provided by local talent. Sometimes one person or several persons would give presentations in a number of districts. Christmas was always very special with Santa Claus appearing with his sack of candies and oranges.

During the year, spelling matches or ciphering matches were held for added incentives.

The people of these communities were closely knit, each helping the others with such jobs as harvesting, butchering, carpenter work or whatever needed several hands to do the work. They supported each other in times of illness and death. There was no TV and little radio so the people had to be self-sufficient when it came to entertainment.

I do not know how much the children learned that winter, but I do know it was a great learning experience for me. The next year I started teaching second grade in the Lewis schools, where I taught 4 years. I was married and had a family. I quit my teaching until we had 4 children in college at one time which included a pair of twins. Then I renewed my certificate and got a job teaching first grade in Greensburg, Kansas. Later

I set up a grade school library and was librarian. I taught a total of 23 years which I enjoyed very much. All five of our children are teaching or in the teaching field as well as two daughters-in-law, also one grand-daughter.

I still feel it is the most rewarding profession in which to be engaged. You as a teacher can affect the thinking of these children. Later on these children grow up to be the leaders of our country. What other job offers such a challenge? To interest children in the great worlds of information that lies before them can be very exciting.

Breitenbach School

An Integrated School

Don Geyer

Kansas City, Missouri

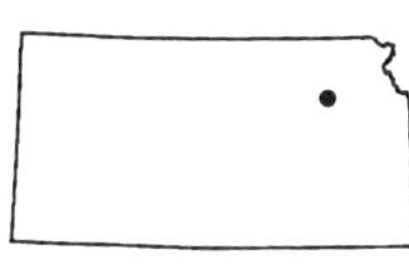

Shawnee County

Kelsey School, District 99 - 1935-36

1/2 mile east of Oakland on Belmont Road

Kelsey school had a fine teacher but could not be rehired because of the NRA regulations requiring that a married woman whose husband had a job could not retain hers. I got the job because I was an "area" young man, married, had a teaching certificate and wanted a job.

I learned a lot real fast about teaching. There were 18 pupils and all eight grades. Five pupils were black. This school presented no problem for Brown vs. Board of Education!

My contract for nine months at $70.00 per month with $5.00 added for doing the janitor work. This was a district serving the rural area

Kelsey School

between the Kaw River and Billard Airport. This was called Topeka Municipal at that time.

There were three board members: Mrs. Arch Roe, director, white and Protestant. Two of her children were pupils. Mr. Charles Patzell, Treasurer, Catholic, sent his children to Catholic School. He owned a Nursery. Mr. H.C. Bryant, Clerk of the board for 23 years, he had no children, was black and farmed the bottom land which produced some of the best melons and they often appeared on our porch when he was on his way to town. He was probably the most dedicated board member one could have.

The school bell was a huge one in a tower and could be heard for nearly a mile. It always rang 1/2 hour before nine and at nine to begin classes. One snowy winter day at nine, all pupils were present and inside so I didn't bother to ring the bell. Mr. Bryant didn't hear the bell and was worried that the teacher may not have made it to school and walked through the snow to make sure all was well. It was. It was a great community with all cooperating and I got another job the next school year at Overbrook, Kansas.

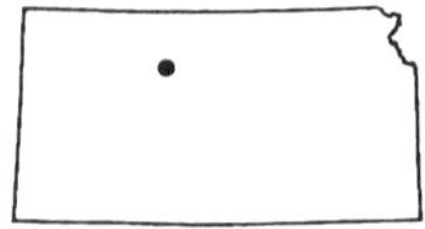

Rooks County

Catches Chickens and Lands a Job

Helen Martin Hulse

from an interview by Carol Parker, courtesy of Fort Hays State University

Twin Mounds School - 1937-38

I wrote a letter (to the school board) to see if they were interested in me at Twin Mounds and followed my letter with a personal appearance because it was so close to the start of school. I had not planned to teach that year, but my love life went on the rocks, and I decided to be a teacher. It was just a month before school started, so I asked the County Superintendent what schools needed teachers and that was the one. So one Sunday my mother drove me around to see the school board. They called me the next day to tell me I had the job. Mr. Stamper said I had his vote right off. When we drove up to his farm, there was a real storm coming up. They were in the yard catching chickens. I laid down all my paraphernalia and helped them catch the chickens! He said, "Anyone who will help me catch my chickens gets my vote!"

The school's name came from the two mounds located in the area that appeared very much alike (twin-like) from a distance.

We had 8 windows, four on each side. I thought we had to decorate our windows for every season. We changed them every week. I thought the windows had to be just alike, so we all made the same pictures to put in the windows. We'd raise the windows and prop them open with little sticks for air conditioning.

I was just about as green about box suppers as I was about teaching in a one-room schoolhouse. I'd never been to a box supper, but I thought we needed a piano. Here we were in the last year the school would be open and I wanted a piano! So we had a box supper to raise money to buy the piano. I got my piano from the American Legion for $25.00, and they delivered it, too! Then it had to be tuned, and I already used my $25.00. I really don't think my school board thought I needed that piano, and now as I look back, I know I didn't! I really don't know what happened to the equipment and supplies after the school closed. I've often wondered about my piano.

Teaching on the Pottawatomie Reservation

Christina Thompson Bowers

Delia, Kansas

Jackson County

Neive School on the Pottawatomie Indian Reservation - 1933-38

I lived three miles from school so didn't have to board. I drove a 1927 Chevrolet Coupe when I could drive and rode a horse or walked when I couldn't drive. Three miles of thick mud or three miles of snow filled roads at times prohibiting the driving of a car. One winter it started snowing and blowing on a Friday and by Sunday the roads were closed. My uncle, Lynn Keller, sent his brother-in-law to get me on horseback. In some places we couldn't guess where the road was. We traveled largely "as the crow flies" riding our horses over fence rows and snow drifts. I was almost too cold to walk when we got off the horses. My aunt was frying "homegrown" hamburgers. Never since have I tasted any quite so good as they were that night. My uncle lived $^1/_2$ mile from school and had four children in school.

I signed my first contract for $35.00 a month. An Indian school in one of the Dakotas closed and several families brought their children home. When it came time for my first check I had 38 students enrolled in school. There were three school board members and they agreed that I should have at least $1.00 a head so they paid me $40.00 a month. I have an old school directory from 1933-34 that shows six people were being paid $35.00, one got $30.00. The rest ranged from $40.00 to $75.00 in Jackson County. There were 103 rural school teachers in Jackson County that year. These were all eight month school years. The highest paid nine month teacher was $170.00 to Mr. Bahred, Principal at Circleville. I had as high as 43 children enrolled over the five years I taught there with more than half of them Indian.

Memories! I enjoyed every minute of it then, but would not want to do it now.

Came Into Power with Hitler and Roosevelt

Wilmer Piper

Topeka, Kansas

Adams - 1933-34; Pleasant Grove - 1935-36; Prest-Linneman - 1938-41

Mr. Piper's memories are included in the Kansas book because of his long tenure teaching in Topeka, Kansas.

I came into power the same year as Hitler and F.D.R. When one teaches in a one-room school, he is the Legislative Department, Executive Department and Judicial Department. However, he has to be the floor sweeper and fire maker also. In my first year of teaching I received $50.00 a month for eight months for a total of $400.00. I commuted the three miles on dirt and I mean dirt roads in a '26 Model T roadster which I bought from my cousin for $45.00. When the roads were impossible, I rode horseback. I had 23 students that year, five of whom were from one family and attended only a day or two a month. In that family of five, a 15 year old girl (turned 16 in December) was in the 4th grade. I was 19 years old. A 12 year old girl was in the 3rd grade and a 14, 9 and 6 year old were the first grade. Another family had five pupils there. The oldest boy was 15 and 6 feet tall. All of them were smart enough but were not regular in attendance.

In the year 1935-36, at a different school, I got $60.00 per month with only six pupils in five grades. There were several days when the weather was bad and I had no pupils.

After I graduated from college in 1938, teaching at Prest, I received $85.00 per month and the next year $87.50. A couple of years ago, Clifford Prest from that school and his wife visited us. He is now in his 60's. My wife thought that I must not have taught anything, for all he could talk about was the hockey box I had made and how much fun it was and our rubber horseshoe games that we played inside in winter. He was a good player and we often had all four shoes on the peg at the same time.

One advantage of a one-room school was for every student to get to listen and watch as others recite. If poems were recited the younger kids got to hear them year after year. Younger ones can be attempting to work upper grade arithmetic problems at their seats. They also can listen to words being spelled. I can still recite all of those poems.

Every Friday, after last recess, we had some type of game or match as we called it. We chose up sides and made a contest out of it. It was usually spelling, arithmetic or geography. Sometimes it was a guessing game. One side would put a word on the board with every other letter being a blank, the others were to fill in the missing letters.

I have fond memories of those days but prefer modern times.

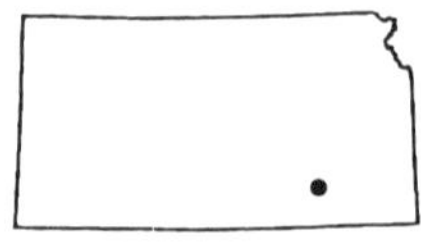

Elk County

What Does "What" Mean?

Alberta L. (Liebau) Young

Howard, Kansas

Oak Grove (Cracker Box) School - 1931-33; Fairview School - 1933-35; Rock Creek School - 1937-41; Consolidated I - 1941-42; Pleasant Plain - 1942-43; Antioch School - 1945-47

Oak Grove School in Elk County was located near the railroad tracks and 160 highway. It was not located near a house. I just had five students from two families, four boys and one girl. I was 17 almost 18 years old. We were eating our lunches outside and a couple of salesmen drove up. They didn't know who was the teacher.

At this same school I kept having a visitor break in at night — a tramp. In those days you did all your own janitor duties. A man up the road heard about the break-ins and said he would check the school and build the fire before I arrived. He also wrote a poem about the happenings. I am sorry I did not keep the poem. I just taught there two years. In those days the teacher stayed two years and moved on to another school. Usually there were 25 to 30 applications. There were three board members and you had to interview. You also had to go to each one to obtain your salary each month. I started out at $75.00 a month. The next year I received $65.00 because poorer districts did not have much money. My next school I received $47.50 a month. They were only eight month terms.

Another experience I remember was at the close of school at Fairview. All eyes were on me as they had put away their books, picked up their papers and were ready for dismissal. I sat down and my chair fell all to pieces. I sat on the floor. The children really had a good laugh!

In those days we had programs and box suppers to raise money. The library consisted of a large dictionary and a set of the Book of Knowledge. I remember one small boy held up his hand one day as he studied the dictionary. He wanted to know what "what" meant. He is an editor today. I still do not know what "what" means.

I had a total of 12 years, all spent in Elk County. They were good years and we turned out good students. The big ones looked out for the little ones. I believe it was hearing some facts over and over that helped. Students also prepared for tests in the 7th and 8th grades. You had to average 80%, I believe.

I taught 36 years, 2 years in 3rd and 4th grades at Grenola, 22 years at Severy, 16 years as a 2nd grade teacher and 6 years as a Reading Teacher.

I started with Normal Training and ended with my Masters Degree. This was summer school, night classes, correspondence and appointed classes.

Taught 42 Years In Kansas

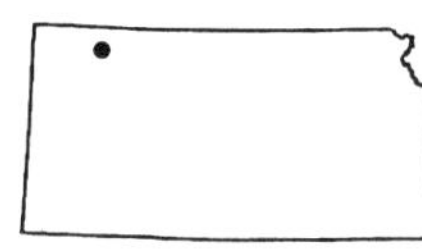

Dale Fisher
Oberlin, Kansas

Decatur County

College Hill School - 1934-35; Center School - 1935-38
Heller School - 1938-39; Cedar Bluffs School - 1939-42

I first held a First Grade County Teaching Certificate. I taught a total of 42 years. I enjoyed my one-room teacher years the most. I only received $40.00 per month my first year.

After my country school experience I was principal at Selden School at Selden, Kansas for one year. This was followed by three years as elementary principal at Atwood, Kansas. This was from 1943-46. I was in college from 1946-48. During 1948-49 I was elementary principal at McDonald, Kansas. I returned to college for the 1949-50 year. After that, a return was made to McDonald. I served as elementary principal for 19 years and principal and superintendent for 10 years.

Students Choose Name for their School

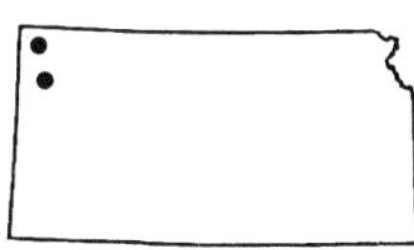

Faye Blue
Goodland, Kansas

Cheyenne County
Sherman County

from a taped interview by Lori Price
Courtesy of Fort Hays State University

Cheyenne County: ***Higland School,- 1936-39, Lawn Ridge, Pleasant Hill - 1934 Dist. 42***

Sherman County: ***Sodtown - 1941, 1944, Hillside School - 1948-70; Neville - 1943***

This school was just called District 6 and ought to have a name. I asked the children to talk with their parents and see if they could come up with some names. Several of them did bring some names. We put them on the blackboard, and then hid our eyes and voted. Hillside was the one that won.

We had one problem the first few years I taught. There were so many rattlesnakes one year, I killed several rattlesnakes on the playground. I killed the first one with a ball bat, after that I kept a hoe.

The Christmas program was always very special. I always gave my presents under the tree to the kids that night, and they gave me mine.

We went on several hikes, sometimes just down to the Beaver a ways, and built a fire and roasted some weiners. We built it down there in the sand where we knew it wouldn't get away.

We would go to Burlington to skate. We rode back to Goodland on the Rocket. The parents drove down there to get us all off the Rocket — this was the passenger train that ran through here.

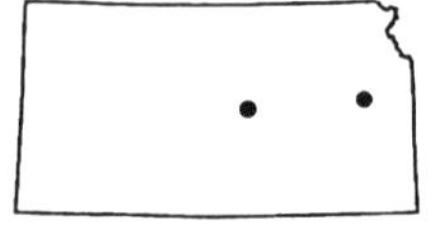

Osage County
McPherson County

A Signed Contract at 16

Ruth Dunn Criss
Topeka, Kansas

Towhead School, Dist. 9 North of Carbondale - 1934
Lee Summit - 2 miles south of Melvern - 1942-44
Highland - 2 miles north of Melvern; Kentucky or Train

I began my career as a teacher when I graduated from the Normal Training course at Burlingame in 1934 at the age of 16. When I was 12 years old I was asked to apply at Towhead School District #9, north of Carbondale, when in four years I would be ready to teach. I was only 16 when I signed my first contract. I started to teach at Towhead School at a salary of $40.00 per month. I boarded with Mr. and Mrs. Pollard for $15.00 a month. Towhead was a rural school with all 8 grades and 18 pupils.

In 1934, the social studies program came into existence in Kansas. I only had the Sears catalog to use for reference, so I taught a course of economics using the catalog.

I did so well that first year that I was asked back for the next year. They said they could not hire me as I was a married woman. I had married Verlin Criss in the course of that year. He was also a teacher at Old Olivet but did not lose his job because he was a married man!

In 1940, World War II started for us. In 1942, teachers were scarce as our young men had gone to war and I was asked to begin teaching again. I took the state exams and was given a two year certificate to teach. I taught at Lee Summit, two miles south of Melvern for two years from 1942-44. Once I was caught in a flooded roadway and was rescued by a farmer with a long hay rope and a big white horse that pulled my Model A Ford backwards out of the flood. That school closed due to low enrollment and I went two miles north of Melvern to teach for five years at Highland School. Times were hard so I began to have a carnival every year to raise money to make it possible for the children to have a hot bowl of soup each day during the cold months. The children took turns under my supervision cooking the soup on an old kerosene cook stove. So cooking was added to the curriculum. I invited the mothers to come on Friday afternoon to take an art class with the children. I believed in a beautiful school full of children's art.

I took the children at this school on geological digs every year as we had a wonderful place to dig about a mile from us. We found trilobites there and many more marine fossils. Every spring we drove to Topeka to see the state capitol and the Historical Society building and sometimes we visited the legislature.

In 1950, we moved to McPherson County and I left my dear eight grade country school to go to work as a 5th and 6th grade teacher at Galva. I loved these children who were mostly Mennonite. I brought the children of my class to Topeka by train to see the capitol. This was the first time the Mennonite children had ever left McPherson County. These children were expected to quit school after eighth grade and learn the trade of farming and the girls to be good homemakers and wives.

I then taught an eight grade rural school called Kentucky or Train School. This school had a large enrollment of 25 students and they were a highly intelligent group. I brought First Aid training in as part of this curriculum. I was accidentally knocked down while playing "King on the Mountain" on a very cold day in December and I broke both wrists. Due to their training, the children knew what to do in such an emergency. They called for the doctor and did all the things I had taught them to do in case of shock.

My County Superintendent, Vinnie Linbeck, asked me to be principal of a school near McPherson, Kansas. Four schools had been consolidated and the school was called Crestview. I had to teach grades five through eight. We had monthly meetings with a great smorgasbord and a movie or a speaker. I went to one boy's home to teach him as he was too ill to come to school that year. The family was so grateful to me.

I taught some very intelligent and worthy children and many have become well known in their chosen fields. I lost some boys in the Vietnam War. That was hard to take. One of the boys was from Train School. He had learned to read sitting on my lap. He was my only first grader. He had a desk but liked my lap better.

Ruth Dunn Criss

In 1959, we moved to Shawnee County and I taught in District 501 for 23 years at Lowman Hill Elementary school.

The things that many children remember about me was that I was fair and that I cared and expected them to be the same. I enjoyed all the children and to this day miss them. Today, if you asked me what I would like to be if I could start all over agin, I would say, "a teacher of children."

Alone

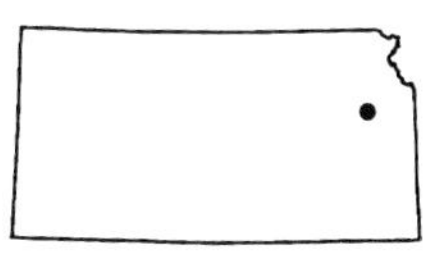

Elizabeth Baker
Ottawa, Kansas

Douglas County
Rock Creek School

I taught four years in three rural schools before I married and had three children who all attended a rural school. In October of 1959, I returned to teaching in a rural school. I enjoyed it very much. The rural families were complete and very cooperative. It was not an easy life as the teacher was also the janitor, recreation leader, mother, nurse, judge, etc. at the school.

I will never forget the night I spent alone in the small rock schoolhouse of Rock Creek, located in the southwest corner of Douglas County. In 1934-35 I was living with my parents and drove my old Ford car seven miles to the school every day on the dirt roads. The school was near the Rock Creek and not near my home. One early winter day I left my car at the schoolhouse and crossed on the logs over the creek to reach a home in the district. I had been invited to spend the night. There were no pupils there. It was a cold, stormy night and I slept very little in the cold upstairs room. I decided "no more of that" so later when the weather was very cold and wet, I took some large blankets, extra food, and a flashlight to school. I told my parents that morning not to worry if I did not come home that evening as I would sleep on the large recitation bench in the schoolhouse. Of course, there was no telephone in the small building and no electric lights or water. The toilets were in the back yard. I carried in extra buckets of coal to keep the large stove going all night. No person in the neighborhood knew I spent the night in the schoolhouse.

Teaching During the Depression

Ella Aley
Topeka, Kansas

Shawnee County
1934-37

I attended a one-room school three years from 1922-25 and taught a one-room school for three years from 1934-37.

The school I attended was Benham School, District 38, Shawnee County located on the northwest corner of the intersection of East 29th and Croco Road. At that time it was called the Red Line Road because all the telephone poles were belted with a red line.

Years after I began teaching I remember hearing the teacher of Benham School hold forth on the values found in a one-room school: "Where else in the world," she asked, "after a week of inclement weather forced indoor recesses, would you find an eighth grade boy square dancing with a first grade girl and treating her with the respect you would expect among young adults?"

In those days playground duty was never a problem. Either the teacher was with the children every minute playing games as a valued player and supervisor, or more, was the rule. If the teacher did not take the playground seriously and used this recess to grade papers, plan lessons or as break time, he or she moved about a great deal.

The children worked on their own getting help only between classes. They soon learned to be sure what the assignment was before they started, for they might have to wait for help. Children learned to tune out everything but their own work. Free time could be used in reading, drawing or other pastimes, but best of all was listening to other classes. If fractions or long division was hard for you, listening into a new class could be helpful to your own understanding and if you were a little kid smart beyond your years, what a delight it was to listen to the older children and dream of the time you would be there yourself.

Not always, but where all was well, the children learned compassion for the smaller and earned self respect for themselves by giving help when needed.

A story from Priddy School, District 66, Shawnee County, was of a teacher named Lacy from Western Kansas. Each year in the spring she would have the children bring firefighting equipment to school. They would set a back-fire and put it out. They then would burn off the schoolyard, prairie style. This got rid of the weeds and brush and left a good stand of grass. Also a good story!

Pie suppers were a way of making money. Each family brought a pie or cake which was sliced and sold for a nickel a slice. This gave money for special supplies. The children put on a program for entertainment. The teacher or someone else furnished the coffee and lit the coal oil lamps after trimming the wicks, polishing the chimneys and filling the oil cavity.

I started teaching in the depth of the depression. Nobody had extra money. I called our evenings "Depression Suppers." Everybody came, everybody ate and nobody paid. Everybody liked that!

Excerpts from a Diary

Kept by J.G. McAntee

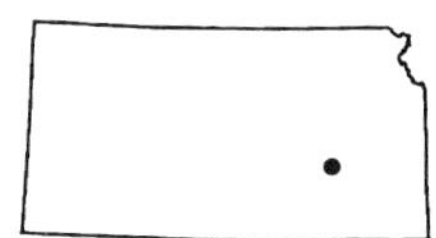

Lyon County
Pretty View #51

November 5, 1935
11:00 a.m.

School just got started. Betty got thrown off horse and was unconscious. Sent Marylouise after car. She went home, George came and we took her home. Still unconscious when we got there. Didn't know me. Kept calling for her mana. Roads awful slick.

April 17, 1935

The day after the night before and the last day — a pick up program and a good one. Such a crowd as had never been. Everybody had a good time I think. Farewell to old #51 — Goodbye!

Program

Song - Spring............................4 School Girls
Reading...Blaine Sells
Solo...................................Thomas Anderson
Song...Holmesburg
Song...School
Piano Duet...............................Riggin Sisters
Reading..Louis
Solo...Miss Watson
Violin...Jake Sells
Tap Dance........................Stalfer - Smnelling
Song, Jack Horner..................Casebier Girls
Quartet...............................Duck Greek Boys

J.G. McAntee

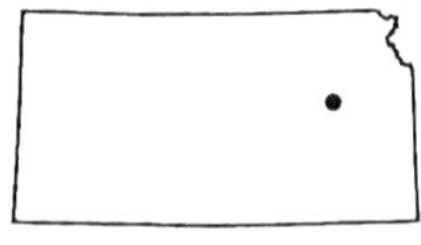

N.E. Wabaunsee County

Poor Choice of Words

Kenneth Keller
Topeka, Kansas

Seeley School, District 33 - 1937-38

I had twenty-one students, at least one in each grade for an 8 month term. The last day of school picnic was cancelled on April 26, 1938, because of a blizzard. We always played baseball, even in the snow. Sometimes we played one-O-cat if not enough wanted to play baseball. Then there were those terrifying county exams that the seventh and eighth graders had to take. There were always one or two non-learners who failed but had to continue in school until their 16th birthday. Kids at recess always hung around the teacher's desk. I was barely 20 years old when I taught this one-room school. I do not know who was more frightened, the children or me. They had never had a man teacher before, and I had never been in a one-room school before.

One rainy recess I was opening mail at my desk, and one of the eighth grade girls standing by my desk asked, "What would you do, Mr. Keller, if one of us kids didn't mind you?" I playfully brandished my letter opening pocket knife and said, "I would probably slit your throats." At 8:00 p.m. that evening I received a telephone summons to the home of the school board president where all three members met me, not smiling. They asked about my threatening the children. I had no idea what they were talking about until the pocket knife was mentioned. Needless to say, I chose my remarks with a little more care thereafter.

This was a prosperous German farm community across the Kaw river south of St. Marys. I did not know about state aid for schools until my frugal board asked me to inquire about the possibility of our being eligible. We were not eligible because the mill levy had to be 3 mills or more, and our levy was 1.19 mills.

I was paid $50.00 per month. I lived with the Seeleys for $10.00 per month board, room and laundry. I walked one-half mile along the creek to school and built a coal fire in the big pot bellied stove with a shield around it on winter mornings. It was easy to save money. I bought a

1929 Plymouth Coupe with wire wheels for $135.00 and had a raccoon tail attached to the radiator cap.

These are the things I remember.

Takes Train to School

Atchison County

Mary McNerny Lykins
Atchison, Kansas

Irish Point School, District 67 - 1938-39

Oak Mills, District 24 - 1939-42 Cummings, District 55 - 1942-43

Each Monday morning at 6:00 a.m., I would take a train to Oak Mills, Kansas at a cost of 25 cents. The taxi to the train cost 10 cents. During the winter months, I would visit with the Postmistress at the Post Office until light enough to walk to school. I lived with a family a mile away, so I got plenty of exercise. These were WWII days, and our school participated in the Atchison County scrap drive. We netted $25.71 for scrap collected and used the money to buy library books. This was the start of rationing, and teachers were given the chore of issuing the first rationing books. This led to my retiring from teaching and accepting a job at the War Price and Rationing Office in Atchison. This 12 month position won me over from an 8 month teaching position.

I loved my years spent in the rural schools and cherish all the memories.

Oak Mills School

Irish Point School

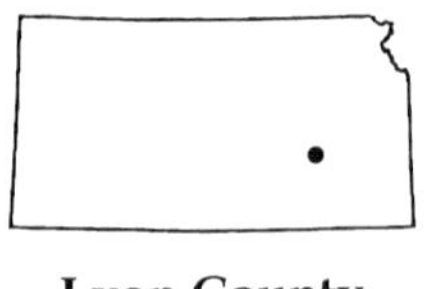

Lyon County
1936-41

The Challenge

Helen Jenkins Brown
Fairland School, District 56; Muttonhead School
Cottonwood School

I taught in Lyon County, 1936-41. My first year of teaching was at Fairland School located 11 miles north and one mile east of Emporia, District 56.

There were 11 students enrolled and I received $45.00 a month for an eight month term. I held a Life Certificate when I first started. I paid $15.00 a month for board and room Monday through Friday. We had a nice fall but one day the temperature dropped 30 degrees and the sky became dark. I went to the coal shed to get more coal and the door blew shut and locked me in. This was after school and I was alone. I took chunks of coal and stacked them up until I could go head first out through a window. I always propped the door open after that.

One of my students had an open palate. This child could read but the mother refused to get help.

I then taught Cottonwood School, four miles west of Emporia. I got $70.00 per month and had 28 students in all eight grades. This was one half mile from Friends Church and cemetery. The teacher put on programs for the church. In 1937, commodities were distributed for hot lunches. I got an aluminum kettle from my mother and a coal oil stove. I fixed hot lunch in the girls' coat closet. One commodity in February was corn meal. One mother thought I should bake cornbread so I got a one burner oven. Then I had to bake the cornbread to go with the soup. I would bake part of this at recess.

I had one little girl who could really run. She said, "You can't catch me." I tried to catch her and stepped into a gopher hole. I broke my foot and tore ligaments in my knee. The big boys were playing Annie Over. They stopped their game and made a chair with their arms and carried me in the school. It was around December 7th, and the next day we were supposed to go into Emporia and see Dicken's "Christmas Carol". I took the children. Sometimes my father took me to school, but I usually drove with one foot until I got the cast off.

I had one boy about 14 years old who gambled and had a gun strapped under his shirt. He had run off a previous teacher. I won him over by hiring him to sweep after school. He was a great help and I paid him $5.00 a week. One day a salesman stopped by the school with undesirable intentions. This boy came out and ran him off. He passed the County exams.

One first grade child came to school on April Fool's Day and asked if I wanted some candy. It was a chocolate covered onion set. My mouth had a terrible taste all day. Her mother had helped her make them.

We had community meetings once a month. The teacher had to put on plays and also a Christmas program.

In 1939-41, I taught Muttonhead School, located about 14 miles southeast of Emporia. I received $75.00 per month. We had community meetings here and I usually put on two plays a year. I usually had between 16 and 20 students. Mr. Williams was an itinerant music supervisor. We were getting ready for a Halloween party and Mr. Williams asked a student to climb up and drive a nail. He could not because it was a religious holiday.

One big boy moved into the district and wanted to make me kneel by locking fingers. He could not make me kneel and it really made him mad. My fingers were so sore after that. I did not ring the bell until after he gave up.

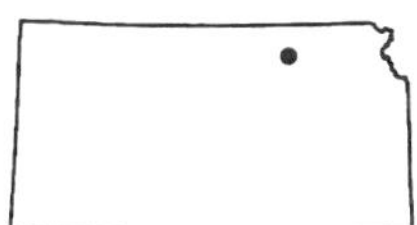

Marshall County

Martha Kirk
Topeka, Kansas

I taught rural school seven years in Marshall County. I did not shovel paths to the outhouse. I did well to clear the front steps.

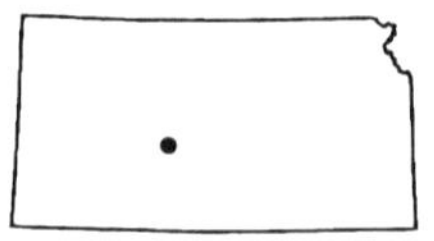

Barton County
St. Catherine
Dist. 98, 1938-42

Dominican Sister Makes a Homemade Duplicator

Sister Dorothy Felder

from an Interview by Beverly Haselhorst
Courtesy of Fort Hays State University

The schoolhouse in which I taught was built in 1921. It was a public school called District #98. The people had completed a new church and the old church was used as the first public school. Lay teachers were the first teachers, but later the people were concerned about the spiritual education of their children. After the public school term would end, the children would attend 2 or 3 months of Catholic instruction in the new church. The education was given by lay teachers. In September, 1921, the pastor secured Dominican Sisters from Great Bend as teachers for St. Catherine's new school, and they have zealously provided the Catholic instruction and education in the parish since that time.

I made my own duplicating material and that was made by purchasing a bottle of liquid chemicals and then pouring it into a pan, such as a cake pan, the larger the better. This liquid stiffened and then you would use a purple indelible pencil and do the writing. You wrote out your test or whatever you were going to give the child and lay that on this gelatin type of material and then it would come off but it was a slow process. You would do one sheet at a time, and let it set for a few minutes and run off another sheet until you got the required number you wanted for your students. I made my own flash cards, charts, and vocabulary words for reading. There was no way of purchasing any of these materials so I made my own.

The school had graduation exercises. The students received their class rings in the 8th grade, a diploma, and a ribbon. It was a big affair. It meant a lot to the children in the 8th grade.

Teachers were expected to conduct themselves according to the ethics and morals. I was a nun, a religious, from the Sisters (Dominican) at Great Bend so I followed my religious decorum of teaching.

Grandpa Fishburn's History Lesson

Mabel R. Gilliland
Ottawa, Kansas

Douglas County
Brubaker School

One of the memories I have is of Brubaker School, in rural Douglas County. In an effort to involve older people of the community in the school, as well as to provide a change in Kansas history approach as Kansas Day neared, I invited Grandpa Fishburn to reminisce with the children about his youth in Douglas County, so many years before.

"It was one of my more inspired ideas," I reflected, as I watched the old man that day. Broad shouldered, though stooped with the weight of his more than ninety-five years, he had stage presence and his voice was surprisingly strong. He held the students — and me — enthralled as he told about his childhood in a log cabin on the prairie, his days in the first old Brubaker School building, and his adventures with his schoolmates.

Every ear was attentively attuned to his voice, and every eye was fixed in rapt attention as he spoke of the remnants of buffalo herds he had seen, tales of the deer hunting, the winter trapping, and the hardships which kept him away from lessons except for a month or so during winter. He held his audience well.

But interest deepened ever more, if possible, as he told of the migration of the Chippewa and Muncie tribes, from the north to their southern wintering place in the not far away Chippewa Hills. A most friendly group of Indians, they would work their way down from the Dakotas to Twin Mound to the northwest of Brubaker, down the banks of the Kaw, the Appanoose, and finally down into the Chippewa Hills. They lived off the land, he related — taking what they could find, be it deer, raccoon, an occasional buffalo, or a settler's cow. A master yarn spinner, we could see it all, dramatically spread out before us.

Another thing they took, he told, was an occasional child. He explained graphically that if an Indian family lost a child, they lost a treasure — on which, if they could not replace it naturally, they would replace by "adopting" one that they found along the way. His voice dropped and every child shivered as he told of a boyhood chum who had been so spirited away — to be rescued only in the next year when the band traveled through on their way north.

He told, too, of sitting in that very schoolroom, in that very spot, and of looking up to see an Indian staring through the window, watching — probably — the children at their books, but at least watching the children. He told how they would hear the rattle of dinner pail lids in the outer coat room, and how the schoolmaster and the biggest boys would have to rush out to rescue lunches, or the students would have nothing to eat until they were home that evening.

But only the master and the biggest of the boys went, he cautioned, for if a small child were caught out, he or she might be abducted. For this had been the fate of his boyhood chum, he revealed. . . never returning from a trip to the frozen outhouse far in the corner of the schoolyard.

He told old tales, well spun by a master spinner, and with the lick of credibility that made them so believable. Old tales of old days, in the times before Kansas became a state; old tales of old days, campfire tales, the shuddery, shivery, delicious kind of tales we all enjoy.

I felt smug and self-satisfied with my Kansas presentation. It had been a great success and I congratulated myself. The children had seen their community and their state through a vastly different, non-textbook perspective.

Until the next day.

In the middle of a recitation a small noise brought deathly quiet to the entire classroom, a small noise which could be only the stealthy rattle of a dinner pail lid from the outer coat room. Twenty-odd gasps cut the silence. Twenty-odd pairs of frightened eyes stared at an equally startled teacher, and then swung as one to the windows and to the rear door separating the classroom from the noise.

Indians? child-snatchers? Were all accounted for? Was any child outside? In spite of myself, I could feel the unspoken questions as plainly in my own heart as I could see them reflected in the eyes of my pupils.

As I stood quietly, so did the three eighth grade boys. As silently as deer stalkers, with no need for direction as the noises in the outer room continued, we armed ourselves with a poker, a broom, a coal bucket, a chunk of firewood. Together we made our way quietly to the door. No word was spoken, no child seemed even to breathe.

As I flung open the door and we burst through it, the poor old hobo who was pilfering food from a lunch pail shrieked, as if set upon by devils. At the sight of our upraised weapons he threw the dinner bucket across the room, yelled like a banshee and tore through the outer door toward the relative safety of the open road, his longing for freedom evidently far overpowering his need for food.

And we? We were too far shaken to argue with his choice of direction, as with quivering limbs we turned back to the classroom — but not to study!

The County Superintendent Helps Out

Mrs. Aurelia Coady
from an interview by Nick Coady
Courtesy of Fort Hays State University

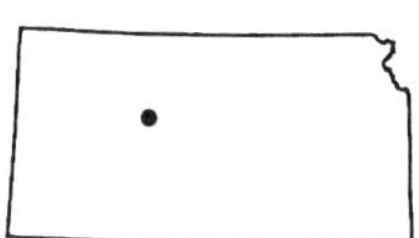

Russell County
Rockridge School
Dist. #72, 1939

Most of the students were of German background. One student in the first grade couldn't speak English when she started school and I couldn't speak German, so we had a little trouble, but she learned. I went to the County Superintendent and he suggested I work on what a chair was, what a table was, and get her to say those things. The County Superintendent, Mr. Hobart Jackson, visited without giving any notice. At first I was kind of nervous over his visit since this was my first year of teaching. He did not reprimand me for any of my teaching. He did mention that he noticed the first grader went up and sat in the waste basket. Now I don't know why she did it that day, but she did. He didn't think that was very good. That was the only eventful part of his visit.

One morning we came up to the school and there was a hobo sleeping in the outside room of the schoolhouse. He knew when we opened the door that we were around, but we didn't stay. The boys and I went down and got one of the school board members that lived 3/4 mile south of the school and got him to come with us. The hobo hadn't done any harm. He evidently just wanted a place to sleep out of the weather.

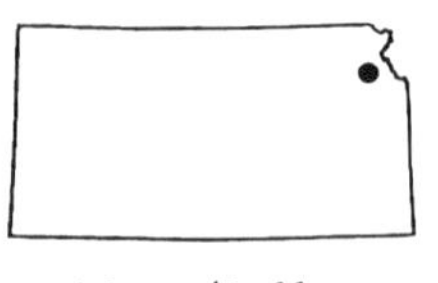

Atchison/Jefferson
County Line

Sugar Bowl Country School

Reba Kenyon Wheeler
Nortonville, Kansas

Hickory Grove School, District J-70-98
"Sugar Bowl" 1940-42

In 1940 the "Sugar Bowl" rural school was reopening after being closed for many years. I was completing Normal Training at Effingham that spring. Because my parents had moved into that district the year before and the school was only a quarter of a mile from our home, I applied for the "Sugar Bowl" school. It would be possible for me to walk to school because I could not afford a car.

The school board hired me giving me $55.00 per month as wages. That was considered a good salary since most Normal Training students were only receiving $50.00 a month. My duties as a teacher required that I keep the schoolhouse neat and clean, carry in the fuel and water, build the fires, keep the snow shoveled off the porch and make a path so the children could get into the schoolhouse easily, teach the children all subjects, covering the entire book in eight months. School started the first Monday in September and closed the middle of April. It took planning and managing to keep the classes interesting and giving each child the attention he needed.

My first day of school was a memorable one. I had made big plans how the day would progress. The day was very normal for the first day of school, because it rained requiring the parents to bring the children to school. I greeted them all at the door. The children came inside and we became acquainted, but the parents stayed outside and visited. When I rang the bell at 9 o'clock all the parents came inside and sat down on the benches that lined the back of the schoolroom. Bravely I led the "Flag Salute" with the children giving me full support. Each pupil was asked to stand and give their name since the children were not acquainted with one another. Then I started assigning lessons for each grade and the parents, satisfied that I was able to handle the school, quietly left the room

— all except one. Each time one mother headed for the door, her small son ran after her crying loudly. She would come back into the room and he would quiet down. I tried to ignore the situation, held classes, answered questions, but the last time she started for the door, I walked swiftly to the back of the room, picked Sylvester up and walked quietly back to his seat. I sat down beside him and put my arm around him and started whispering into his ear that it was nearly time for recess and that we were going outside (the rain had stopped) and have fun playing games. He stopped crying and even gave me a smile. When I went back to my desk and faced that schoolroom of children I saw looks of approval on every face. At that moment I knew that I had a wonderful group of children with which to work.

We had such fun on the playground at recess and noon hour. We played numerous games some of which were: "Two Deep", "Last Couple Out", "Can't Cross My Bridge", "Andy Over", "Blackman's Bluff", "Fox and Geese", and "Ball". On rainy or snowy days when we were unable to play outdoors, we stayed inside playing: "Pussy Wants A Corner", "Upset the Fruit Basket", "I'm Hiding in _____", "Going to Africa" and numerous guessing games.

Soon after school started in 1940, the Polio epidemic caused all Atchison County schools to close for two weeks. I used those two weeks to good advantage, making artwork for Fridays, preparing desk work for the first graders, and finishing the rhythm band equipment that I had started making before school started. (Since the school had been closed some time they did not have any equipment.)

The schedule in the rural school was simple and regular. One morning per week after the "Flag Salute" we would recite Bible verses starting with the letters of the alphabet that we had memorized, report on current events from the newspaper, practice on keeping time and playing the different instruments in the rhythm band, and sing songs. Classes were called to the front of the room and given from 5 to 15 minutes per class. (This depended on the number in the class and the assistance they needed.) After we returned from the playground at noon, I read a chapter from a library book to the school, which they seemed to enjoy. On Fridays we had art and made pretty artwork for the school windows, board and to take home. Sometimes if we had time we had clean-up day on Friday, with children cleaning out their desks, cleaning the erasers and the blackboards.

Each fall the teacher was expected to plan a program and the women of the district furnished food for a jitney supper to make money for school supplies. Besides selling food for the supper, there were cake walks, and guessing games to make money. With the first year's money we purchased rhythm band equipment and it sounded so good compared to my homemade ones.

In 1940 the county recommended "Hot Lunches" for rural school children. Since the only stove in that school was the old "potbellied" stove that stood in the front of the school and was in need of repair, it made a problem. In fact, the school board had informed me that I would be unable to bank the fire at night because there was a large crack in the back of the stove and might cause a fire. So, each morning I came to a cold, icy room. Not being the best fire-maker in the world the pupils and I had to wear our coats until noon some days because it took that stove that long to heat the area. I decided the only way my pupils could have anything hot would be to have each one bring soup in a glass jar and I brought a large kettle from home, poured water in the bottom of it and set the jars in the kettle and on top of that heating stove. It worked and we enjoyed hot soup on cold wintry days.

The school board also informed me when I took the school that the well water was not fit to drink and they would have to have it pulled and cleaned. I carried water from home each morning for drinking water and washing our hands. One hot September day we ran out of drinking water and Bertha and Juanita walked to the Thompsons and pumped and carried back a pail of water. It was quite a walk and the pail was half full by the time they reached the school house, but everyone was most grateful for a drink of water. Sometime later the well was repaired and pumped clean and we were able to have water on the schoolgrounds.

In March of 1941 my parents moved and I had to find some place to stay. My uncle and aunt, Jesse and Mary Van Horn, offered to let me stay with them for $10.00 per month. From that time on I walked $1^1/_4$ miles to and from home each day, never once did I catch a ride. It was an east and west road and always blocked solid when we had a large snow storm. Sometimes I had difficulty wading snowdrifts almost to my hips in places to reach the school house early and get the stove burning to heat that icy schoolhouse.

I soon learned not to leave the pupils' papers in my desk at night. I stayed after school at the beginning of school to grade papers and placed them in the top desk drawer. The next morning when I went to get the papers to pass out, they were badly chewed and a large mouse's nest was found in the corner of the drawer. At our house my dad had always set the traps, baited and emptied them, so it was a new experience for me to set, bait and empty traps, but I learned quickly and soon had the school house free from rodents.

There are so many fond memories of the people of "Sugar Bowl" district. They were good, clean, Christian families, raising their children to have respect, to enjoy the wonders of nature, and appreciate the love of family and friends.

Several of my fondest memories of that neighborhood were: The chocolate covered cookies in a pretty box given to me on "April Fool's Day". They proved to be cardboard covered with delicious chocolate, (the Kramer girls brought those).

A note left on my desk one evening said, "We don't want you to leave, we want you to be our teacher next year. We love you". Signed Vera and Robert (the Ellerman cousins).

The warmhearted families of that district who hosted a lovely shower for me when they found that I planned to be married in 1942.

The lovely iris that Clara Ellerman gave me for my first home which was the beginning of a large iris collection. To date I have close to 100 named varieties in my yard in 1991.

The many former pupils and parents who have kept in touch with me all these years: Geneva Ellerman, Robert and Millie, Juanita Kramer who lives in Connecticut, and Bertha Ellerman are just a few of them.

I have only wonderful memories of the one-room school house.

Hickory Grove J 70-98

Teacher	Year	Salary a Month
Edith Bauer	1914-1915	$40.00
Inez Kleiner	1915-1916	$40.00
Kathryn Wilson	1916-1917	$50.00
Esther Vincent	1917-1918	$50.00
Sylvia Babcock	1918-1919	$55.00
Beulah English	1919-1920	$65.00
Gladys Sowles	1920-1921	$80.00
Gladys Sowles	1921-1922	$80.00
Gladys Sowles	1922-1923	$80.00
Marie Beyer	1923-1924	$80.00
Flo Cunningham	1924-1925	$80.00
Flo Cunningham	1925-1926	$90.00
Flo Cunningham	1926-1927	$90.00
Bertha Cook	1927-1928	$80.00
Bertha Cook	1928-1929	$82.50
Orlena Cook	1929-1930	$70.00
Mattie Wells	1930-1931	$70.00
Mary Gehnder	1931-1932	$70.00
Mary Gehnder	1932-1933	$75.00
Mary McLenon	1933-1934	$45.00
Mary Beadle	1934-1935	$45.00
Clara May Hawk	1935-1936	$40.00
Reba Kenyon	1940-1941	$50.00
Reba Kenyon	1941-1942	$60.00
Bertilla Bell	1942-March 1943	$62.40
Reba Wheeler	March 1943	$75.00

List compiled by Geneva Speck Ellerman, Nortonville, Kansas

My Aunt Lura VanHorn, a former student of Hickory Grove School, had this poem written in one of her books.

We're not crazy
We're no fool,
We got our education
In the Sugar Bowl School.

The Hickory Grove School
(Its legal name)
Sugar Bowl School
(Its nickname, but I never heard it called by any other name.) It received its name "Sugar Bowl" after a gathering when the sugar bowl was stolen.

Reba Kenyon Wheeler
and students
Hickory Grove School - 1941-42
called "Sugar Bowl"

Teacher Passed the Test

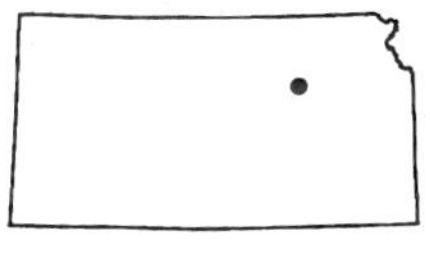

Geary County

Glenna Wilson
Manhattan, Kansas

Reynolds School, Humboldt Creek Road

It was before WWII and the school was just then being wired for electricity. The workers were electrifying the school over the weekend. On Monday morning, I opened the door to find a large black snake with fangs showing, lying on the floor. As I walked closer to the snake, I could see it was electrical wire coiled to look like a snake with the wire exposed to look like fangs. The electricians thought this would be a great joke and told the man I boarded with to stand outside and watch my reaction. This man later told the electrician that the teacher did not run, so I guess I passed the test.

The man and wife I boarded with were an interesting couple. He was from England and she was Swiss. He bought her box supper at a community gathering. She had made a Washington pie, and he thought it was the best pie he had ever tasted and said, "I'm going to marry this girl." And he did. After that every time she baked a Washington pie, he would tell her that was why he married her.

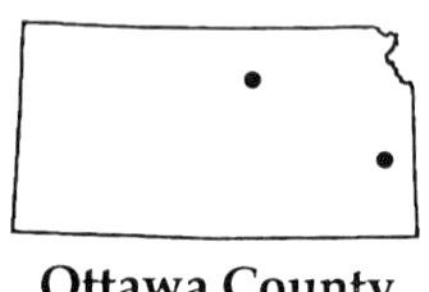

Ottawa County
Linn County

Believes in Memorization

Pauline Gilmore
from an interview by Rex Cooper
Courtesy of Fort Hays State University

Ottawa County — *Crown Point School - 1940*
Linn County — *Crawford School*

I was 17 when I started teaching. I went to high school at Culver. Our senior year we took a course called Normal Training. We had to take a state exam put out by the state. Then I got a Normal Training Certificate, and it was good for 2 years. Then you had to get 8 hours of summer school. This was in 1940. I felt real lucky to get my home school. I taught 2 years at $60.00 a month. The following year I went to Crawford School in Linn County. Everything had raised on account of the war, and then I made $110.00 a month.

I'm from the "old school" and I don't think memorization hurts a thing. I believe you should know where to look and how to look it up. I still think it's all right to have a few things memorized in your head. We had to memorize things to pass those exams and when we had programs, why it would be amazing what the kids could learn of the parts of the play. The little ones would speak a reading and not make a mistake. They'd get up there and say it. The last years I taught, some of the little kids just had 3 or 4 lines and they couldn't say them.

The outhouses were out on the "north forty". The first year I taught, all we had was a Sears and Roebuck catalog. But then in the 1950's we had regular toilet tissue.

In the old country schools, they (8th graders) took those exams at the county seats. All the 8th grade boys and girls would go to the graduation exercises. The boys were all spruced up with new suits and the girls would be in their first high heeled shoes. They would have a program and speech and the kids would all be up there on stage.

Don't Cross a Board Member

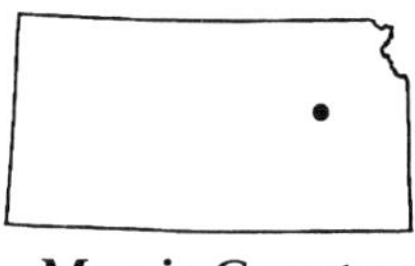

Morris County

Ernie Shawgo Gunzelman

Topeka, Kansas

4 Mile School, South of Council Grove

My first year of teaching was in 1941. I held a 30 hour certificate. I taught 4 Mile School south of Council Grove. I rented a room from Ross Swendson, who was on the school board.

I remember one 7th grade boy that had the reputation of a trouble maker from his previous school. His dad was a bootlegger and was in jail. I won him over by letting him help build the fire. I rode the school board member's horse sometimes, and this boy would ride with me. We became buddies. I believe there were 10 students that year and the school closed at the end of the term for lack of students.

At the end of the first month of teaching I rode my horse over to the school board member's home to pick up my check which I understood would be for $60.00. When he handed me the check it was for $70.00. I told him he had made an error. He looked at me with a very mean look and told me never to tell a board member that he had made a mistake. Then he smiled and told me I had done such a good job the first month that the board had decided to give me $10.00 more a month.

The whole community was called 4 Mile. I guess it was about 4 miles from Council Grove. The parents were strict and always supported the teacher.

One of the highlights of the year was a box supper. If the teacher was single, her box brought a lot of money. The money was used to buy things for the school.

As far as I know the 4 Mile School building is still standing. We always had a prayer at noon and at the end of the day to keep us safe. The students took turns giving the prayer.

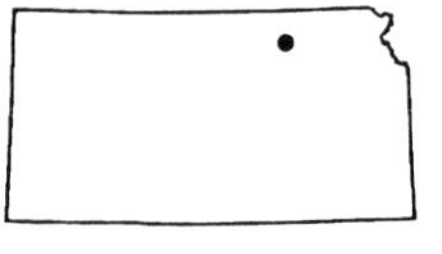

Marshall County

My Own Private School

Eunice Nordquist
Blue Rapids, Kansas

Gallup School - Our Farm
Pleasant Ridge School - near Marysville

I taught English in high school at a town called Irving, Kansas. Irving does not exist anymore. I then taught two years in Waterville, Kansas. After that I went to take nurse's training at Evanston, north of Chicago, Illinois. After six months, I married Charles Nordquist. We owned a home in Waterville and had three children. When the Second World War was over, Charles came home and decided to sell our home and buy a farm. There was a school house on the farm and since we had three kids in school, we decided to keep it open. I taught my own children plus one or two others. When my older girl went to high school in Blue Rapids, we closed the school and sent the two younger children into Blue Rapids, too.

I taught for three years in the Prairie Ridge School north of where we lived and later taught another country school south of town.

Eunice Nordquist

Wonderful Memories

Annie Irene Thompson Canady
Shawnee, Kansas

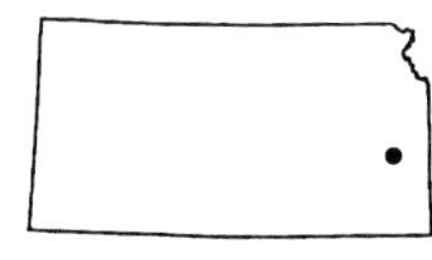

Anderson County

Antioch (Red Star) near Bush City - 1940-41
Salem, near Selma - 1941-42; Waverly near LaHarpe - 1942-46

I started teaching right out of High School. My first school was Antioch (Red Star), Bush City. My salary was $45.00 a month. Out of this came $12.50 a month for room and board and any school supplies that were needed. I had to walk a mile and a half around the road or cut off 1/2 mile if I cut through the cow lot and the woods over a big hill. I was 18 years old and had one eighth grade student who could have caused me a lot of trouble if she wanted, but she was a wonderful girl named Lucille Hall (Davis). I'm sure I learned more than any of the students that year. It was a good year, the students did well and we had some wonderful programs and pie suppers.

I made a mistake when I changed schools for the next year, but the thought of $10.00 a month raise was too hard to resist. That was a lot of money then, almost unheard of. The school was a challenge and I earned my raise. Of course my rent went up to a whopping $14.00 a month. It was a nice school and close.

My next school was Waverly, near LaHarpe. Waverly was a large school with all eight grades and always one that was in between grades and should have been in a special class. That was almost unheard of then, too. I had to walk 1 1/2 miles to school down a country road. It did not take long but if the farmer had bulls in the pasture next to the road, I could have broken the record for the mile I am sure.

After I arrived at school, the first thing was to get the fire started so the room would be warm by the time the students got there. Then I carried water in to fill the stone water cooler. Time to get busy! I then put the work on the chalkboard and any other special things for the day. Yes, I remember the sweeping compound that was used to oil the floors to keep the dust down. What a chore it was to sweep it up but it was all in a day's work. Erasers had to be dusted and blackboards washed. The children usually took turns cleaning the erasers and if one came in with chalk dust on their face, you knew there had been a little horseplay. This was a good school with good students and cooperative parents.

I have many fond memories of the little one-room country school, especially when the little first graders would stand by me to read and forget that I was not mother and ease over onto my lap.

Then there were current events when they all brought something interesting to report. One little boy was holding up his hand to tell his story and he blurted out, "My brother got put in jail." His brother an sister were so embarrassed.

There were so many funny things happened that I could write a book. Not so fond memories of payday, your check had to be signed by all three board members or you could not cash it. I have had to walk across a plowed field to get the farmer to sign, then on to another where you might catch the last one in the house or near the henhouse.

I taught from 1940-46. I might have still been teaching if my husband had not come home from two and a half years over seas. He was one of the first to land in Casablanca, then shipped to Italy where he fought through the Italian Campaign.

Waverly School - 1942-43

Miami County

Who's The Boss?

Della (Dollie) Canady Thompson

East Washington, Garnett - 1944-45
Salem, Dist. 68, Selma - 1945-46

Have you ever thought how it would feel for someone 5 ft. 1¼ in.

tall and 18 years old to come face to face with a young man 5 ft. 11 in. tall and only 16 years old with a build like a football player? Well that is exactly what happened to me on my very first day of teaching in a school where all the children were strangers to me and I to them. This was a little country school near Garnett, Kansas, called East Washington.

This young man was one of my eighth graders at that school. As the children were lined up to file into the room he came up to me and said "Now I guess you know who is going to be boss." I do not know where I found the courage but I reached behind me and took hold of the handle of the ballbat standing in the corner of the cloakroom and replied, "Yes, we do and if I have to use this bat on your head to impress you, then so be it." From that day until the last day of school, I had no problem with that young boy. In fact he carried the coal and the drinking water for me without me even asking him to do so.

When the last day of school arrived this boy was one of the first of my students to come to me and say how he had enjoyed studying and coming to school that year. I have often wondered whatever became of him.

My second year of teaching was in my home school. It was another little country school, Salem School District 68, near Selma, Kansas.

I was going to teach some of my neighbor boys and girls with whom my sisters, brothers and myself had spent many hours playing softball or Blindman's Bluff in summer and Fox and the Goose in winter months. How could I expect them to call me Miss Canady when they had always called me Dollie?

I asked them if it would be easier for them to call me Miss Dollie. They all agreed and this was better, but I must tell you they did forget to put the Miss before my name quite often. I suppose I could have reminded them; however, I could not seem to care enough to correct them. So long as they respected me as their teacher I could see no harm in it.

One of the things I remember about these young boys and girls from both schools, was the way they would study to get their lessons completed by Friday afternoon at 3 o'clock so we could have Spelling Bees or History Contests. These History Contests consisted of using the wall maps of the different countries and their capitals. The boys and girls would have a great time challenging each other to see who could score the highest points. Even the little first graders enjoyed these contests.

We did not have anyone telling us that we could not have prayer to start our day so every morning consisted of the flag salute and a short prayer. I had 3 different religions in this school but not one parent objected to our prayer. After prayer, I would read another chapter from a book the children had picked out from the school library. I honestly believe that this helped to settle the children down and get them ready for another day.

I think we have lost a lot when schools were no longer allowed to have prayer as part of the opening exercise.

Oh yes, before I forget, every one of my eighth graders graduated on the honor roll. How proud I was of those boys and girls.

I saw one of my students a few years later and she was married and had a baby. I WAS FEELING OLDER EVERY MINUTE.

I taught school only 2 years, but if I had to do it over, I would have gone back to school and continued teaching.

I loved every one of these young students and think of them often.

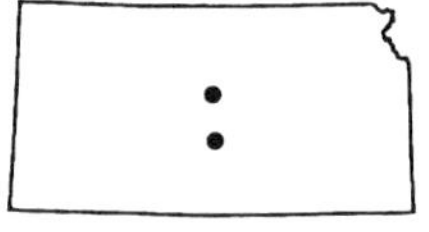

Ellsworth County
Rice County

An Eighth Grade Student Aide

Esther Jarvis
Topeka, Kansas

Ellsworth County — *Trivola School - 1943-44*
Rice County — *Kansas Center School - 1944-45*

Although I graduated from McPherson College with a degree in Elementary Education, the two years I spent teaching in rural schools were the extent of my teaching career. I graduated from high school on May 20, 1943, and signed my first teaching contract the next day on my 18th birthday.

I probably never would have considered teaching a rural school if I had not attended one for a year. I had attended a town school for seven years and then my parents moved to a farm, and I attended my eighth grade in the same school my mother had attended. It was such a pleasant experience that I knew teaching in a "country school" would be both interesting and challenging. I attended Emporia State Teacher's College that summer where I took courses that did little to prepare me to teach. However, the second summer the Dean of the college, with persons in the Education Department had a program planned just for emergency certified teachers. This was a great help, and although it was the hardest eight hours as far as time required I ever had in college, I felt I was ready to go out and teach. Before we were through, we had to have Social Studies Units outlined for the year, correlated with books to read, music, English and spelling.

My first school was Trivola in Ellsworth County and I had seven students in five grades. The previous teacher was an older experienced lady who left to become the County Superintendent of Schools. She left me with a great group of students who were no discipline problems, knew how to study and if they did not like school I did not know it. My salary the first year was $100.00 a month. Out of this I paid one dollar a day for my board and room, repaid my money I borrowed to go to college and saved enough to go again the next summer. That spring I was offered $150.00 to teach at Kansas Center School which was closer to me, so I changed schools. Here I had six students in the first four grades and an eighth grade student who had graduated the year before, but her parents did not think she was mature enough to board away from home when she went to high school. She was a good "teacher's aide" as she played the piano for music, helped the younger students with art, and listened to them read. In turn I helped her with an introduction to freshman English, written composition, and algebra.

Teachers in country school were expected to do all their own janitor work, and therefore I was no different than any other teacher when I carried in coal and drinking water, swept the floor, emptied the trash, emptied the ashes from the heating stove, and went early enough to build the fires. I learned to bank the fires, so the building would not be too cold when I got there in the morning. Both years I boarded about a mile from the school and walked both ways except in the very coldest weather. People in the community would sometimes give me a lift if they happened to be going my way.

One of the highlights of the school year was presenting programs for the parents and others in the community. We gave programs at Christmas and the last day of school and one year we gave one about Halloween. The programs consisted of songs, a short skit or two and readings by everyone from the youngest to the oldest. We practiced during music period, sometimes at recess and during lunch hour. The mother of one of the students played for us the first year since I did not play the piano and came several times to practice with us. The parents and whole community turned out, complete with refreshments as these were social events and a time to visit with neighbors. And the students beamed as they showed off their talents.

Because I am an avid reader and wanted my students to like to read as well, I read to the whole school after lunch each day. The favorites that I remember were about the Cherry Twins (two books) in which each chapter ended in suspense, and they couldn't wait to find out what happened the next day. Other favorites were ***My Friend Flicka*** and ***Thunderhead***.

Some of my reflections on teaching in a country school is that I am glad I started in a country school. Discipline was no problem and the students accepted the fact that they were there to learn and were eager to please the teacher. And at the young age of 18, I was glad I did not start in a town school with my former teachers as my peers.

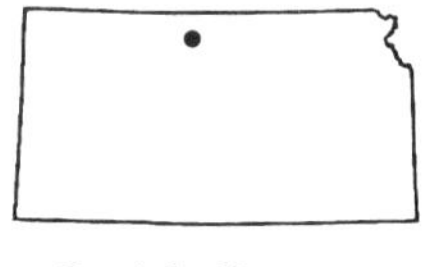

Smith County

Teacher is No Musician

Charles O. Stones
Garden City, Kansas

Oriole School - 1943-44; Mount Hope School - 1947-49

My first school was Oriole in Smith County, located three miles from my parent's home. I took a car to school on the first and last day of school. The remainder of the time I rode either a horse or a bicycle. One day my horse got loose and went home - that day I walked three miles. That year I was 17 years old through February 25th. If there were laws governing beginning age, our school community did not know about them when I started school in 1931. Normal Training was offered for the last time when I was a senior in high school. If you passed the state exam after having had Normal Training you were qualified to teach.

My second rural school, Mount Hope, Smith County was one I had attended as a child. In fact, I attended that school and had the same teacher for eight years. Mr. Ward was a great teacher and mostly because of him I chose to teach. He was a great teacher in all areas except music. The only song I remember singing during those years was "Row, Row, Row Your Boat." There were 36 families in that rural school district when I attended, now there is one family with one person in the family residing in that 9 square mile area. A Friday afternoon treat about once a month was a Geography match, Spelling Bee or an Arithmetic match.

My daily schedule: After the chores at my parents home, I saddled the horse and rode the three miles, carried out the ashes, started the fire, pumped water for the water container, pumped another bucket to warm near the stove for washing, put up the flag and made myself ready to receive the first children at 8:30 a.m. School started at 9:00 a.m. Reading and Arithmetic were taught separately by grade every day as were Geography and English. Health and Penmanship were taught most days to the group. Spelling was a Monday, Wednesday, Friday event unless you got a hundred on Wednesday, then you had the opportunity to read on Friday. Health was very important, though not an every day event. Morning recess always came at 10:30 a.m. for 15 minutes. Lunch started with washing hands, followed by an outside play time for 30-45 minutes. Students returned to their studies at 1:00 p.m. Afternoon recess came at 2:30 p.m. and school was dismissed for the day at 4:00 p.m. After the students had departed and the papers that were absolutely essential had been graded, the building was swept using sweeping compound on the floor. The water container was then emptied, the flag taken down, and coal and cobs were brought in to speed the heating process. On Friday, the students were reminded to take their towel home for washing. Books requiring special preparation for the next day were placed in the saddle bags or bicycle rack and I started for home, not realizing I had fully earned my $4.25 for the day, but rather wondering if I had hurried over something that should have taken more time.

School was held no matter what, because some families had no telephone and no one could take the chance of calling off school in a snowstorm with the possibility of some child walking to school and finding no one there.

One morning while walking to my second school, which was less than three-fourths of a mile from home, in a near blinding snow storm, I almost stepped on a rooster pheasant with snow and ice crusted over its eyes and near exhaustion. I picked him up, placed him inside the sheepskin coat I wore that morning, took him to school, and placed him in a storm cellar on the grounds. After the storm, the door was propped open and three days later tracks in the snow were evidence he had recovered and departed.

I retired after 44 years in Kansas schools.

Lyon County

In Dad's Footsteps

Ray McAntee

Topeka, Kansas

Harmony Hill School, District 89

I graduated from Admire High School in the spring of 1947. Since my dad was a country school teacher and farmer, he suggested I go to summer school at Emporia State Teacher's College, then try teaching school for a year. After I finished eight weeks of summer school Dad introduced me to the County Superintendent of Schools of Lyon County. He told me immediately of a school south of Emporia. Dad knew two of the school board members and on the way out of the courthouse we met one of the members. One week later, two weeks before school started, I became a country school teacher.

The school was Harmony Hill, District 89 located six miles southwest of Emporia. The contract was $175.00 per month for eight months. I still have the contract.

I roomed and boarded with one of the board members. To help pay rent I did farm chores for him. That was not new to me as I grew up on a farm. To get to school I walked 1 1/2 miles each way.

I had fourteen pupils in seven grades. The older children helped the younger ones a lot. I spent most of my time with the one first grader and the three eighth graders. Dad told me to make sure the first grader learned to read and the eighth graders knew enough to pass the county examination in the spring. He claimed if I accomplished those two objectives I would be considered a good teacher. So I taught the eighth graders; they taught the seventh, sixth and fifth. I usually spent the first quarter of the day with the one first grader, two second and two third graders. I don't remember what I had them do in the afternoon. I do remember I spent time with the first grader after lunch because she would get so sleepy.

The county had a music supervisor who visited each school once a week. Also the County Superintendent would visit twice a year. My music supervisor was Mrs. Ruth Lynn. She helped me put on the Christmas program which I appreciated very much. Being eighteen years old, a boy, hardly any education, and being away from home for the first time was a completely new experience for me. However, I knew Mrs. Lynn because she was the music teacher that I had just four years previously while attending a country school in northern Lyon county. She had me sing "Jingle Bells" as the last number so I would be out on the little stage to help Santa pass out treats. Teachers were expected to give each pupil a brown sack of candy that included an orange or an apple. Dad and I bought candy from the Emporia Wholesale Company in the bulk and then sacked it at home the week before the program.

I remember playing in the snow with those kids a lot. We played Fox and Geese, built forts for snowball fights, and rode sleds on the little hill north of the school.

I liked sports and the small town schools had softball and basketball teams. So I decided I would have some ball teams. I took my little country school basketball team to the county tournament. We didn't have suits. We were the only country team in the tournament. I had a mixed team of boys and girls and they got to play on an indoor court. There was a lot of comment about the little country team from Harmony Hill. The parents were just as excited as the kids. I came in contact with one of the girls whom I taught that year, and playing basketball in that big gym was the thing she mentioned first. We practiced on dirt all of the time, so an inside court was a big deal. About ten years ago, one of the boys in my class at Harmony Hill came up to me and said, "Mac, I remember the forts and snowball fights we used to have. My kids can't even throw one snowball here."

So I guess it is all a part of growing up in a different way. On cold days I remember sitting around the big stove with the kids eating soup their mother had sent to school. I warmed it for them on top of the heating stove. We dried the wet mittens and overshoes there.

I do not know where those kids are now. I know I grew a lot that year and got educated by experience. My dad rode a horse to teach school, and I also rode a horse to school during my first eight years of schooling. I wished many times that I would have had a horse the first year I taught. That first year I taught I thought about Ichabod Crane who I had read about in high school. I do not remember what happened if a teacher was sick. I never missed a day in the first twelve years of teaching. The one year I was going to teach turned into forty-one.

10 Consecutive Summer Sessions

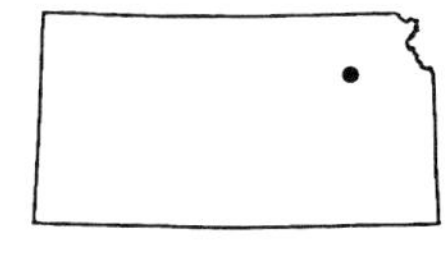

Shawnee County

Elsie Hylt
Topeka, Kansas

Union School - 1944-48; Rice School

Back in the days of rural schools, I think the children got a good basic education and a lot of the fundamentals. In 1944-48, I taught Union School in Shawnee County. I had all 8 grades and 28 students. I took Normal Training in high school. For 10 consecutive summers I went to summer school to get my degree. It was required to get 8 hours each summer. In 1959, I taught Rice School on Norwood street in Topeka.

In the years during World War II, there was a shortage of teachers. I can not remember being short of supplies, but I can remember some of the students being emotionally upset by having brothers or other relatives in the war.

Smoking in the Outhouse

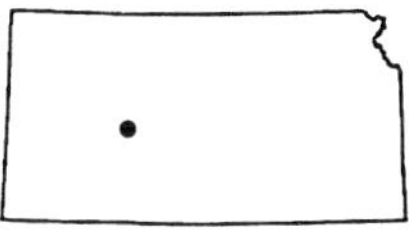

Ness County

Bill Cole
from an interview by Jim Cole
Courtesy of Fort Hays State University

Francis School, Dist. 18 - 1946-49

The first school, District 18, Francis School, was built in 1885 out of stone by my grandfather. Then in 1926, they put up a wooden frame building and it was built by my uncle. This building was sold in the 1960's and moved to Ness City and is still being used as a residence. The original building is still standing.

I lived with different families but I did not stay with families of the school children during the school term. We did quite a bit of reading in the evening when I was boarding in these places. Some evenings we would make candy or play Pitch or Pinochle.

The children at school got along fairly well, but there was quite a bit of feuding in the community. Family feuding between, maybe cousins and whatnot, and this would carry over with the children at school; but the school itself got along fairly well during schooltime. You'd catch some of the boys smoking once in a while behind the out-house or in the outhouse. We also built a cave down by the draw and sometimes you would catch them smoking down there.

The school closed for lack of students and consolidated with another school about 4 1/2 miles east known as Highpoint Center. If you had less than 10 children then the state made you consolidate.

Atchison County
District 42
1947-48

Kept the School in the Family

Bertha Ellerman Potts
Nortonville, Kansas

I had five students in 5 grades when I taught District 42. Needless to say, each class got my undivided attention.

My uncle, Albert Ellerman, was on the school board and I had two of his children in school. The other three lived close by. When the snow drifted the roads shut, I stayed with my uncle and all the children, including me, would walk to school picking our way through the snow.

Putting on a program for the Jitney Supper with only five pupils would seem to be a problem but wasn't. They all learned their recitations and skit parts easily, as well as the songs. Cake walks and drawings for blankets, etc. were some of the activities. Proceeds went for something the school needed.

Playground games were limited with such a small group. They liked to play Andy-over, Tag, London Bridge, Drop the Handkerchief, Hide and Seek, and Fox and Geese in the snow. Inside games played were I Spy and Upset the Fruit Basket.

Janitor work consisted of carrying in coal and cobs for the jacketed stove, keeping the fire going and banking it before I left in the afternoon, sweeping the floors, washing chalkboards and dusting the erasers. I appreciated the nice hardwood floor put on top of the old floor so I didn't have to use sweeping compound - just a dust mop every day.

Then there were the outhouses placed at the far back edge of the yard. They seemed very far away in the cold weather. I had to dry out the small ones sometimes as they hated to go out and waited until it was too late. You had to watch out for spiders and snakes, so it was always a dreaded trip.

The schoolhouse was quite old in 1947, although it had electricity and new hardwood floors. A few years later, the school closed and sold at auction to be moved. My dad was the successful bidder and moved it to his farm to be used as a granary and for storage. Eventually, my husband and I bought the farm and the old schoolhouse is still standing there.

I never had to leave home to teach there, and I never have to leave home to reminisce there to this day.

Bertha Ellerman Potts

Decatur County
Decatur School
1941-43

Teachers Wear Many Hats

Nadine Anderson
Oberlin, Kansas

I enjoyed my experience as a country school teacher. I was only 18 when I started teaching. You were the janitor and everything - pump the water and fill the container. I walked a mile to school each morning and home at night. I only had nine pupils in 5 grades. After two years I taught in a city school for two years and then married.

Rawlins County

Swept Up Enough Dust To Make A Farm

John R. Bearley

Fairview School, District 48 - 1933-34
Achilles School District 14 - 1934-38
Achilles School District 214 - 1946-47

Having graduated from high school in the spring of 1933 and successfully passing the written test to gain a second grade teaching certificate, I began my career at a salary of $35.00 per month. The contract read, "With eight months of school if possible." I was paid an extra $1.50 for hauling five gallons of water which provided the drinking and sanitary needs for 28 pupils and me. The Great Depression had just begun so the pay looked pretty good, but as stated, the board was not sure there would be enough money for eight months of expenses.

I hauled one of the first grade pupils to school as I drove by her home. The transportation was provided by a 1925 Model T Ford coupe which I had purchased for $25.00 just before school started.

My second year of teaching was at a new school. I felt I was worth more than thirty-five dollars a month as a teacher - say fifty; but they could not match my request so move was my lot. Upon visiting with the County Superintendent, he told me there were three vacancies in the county. I told him of my desire for fifty dollars a month and he recommended the school at Achilles. I made my appearance and found there were several others to be interviewed. It turned out I was the last one and negotiations began. I was first offered forty dollars a month, still needed fifty, offered forty-five, still fifty. Finally at about one in the morning and a rain beginning to fall, I signed a contract for $47.50 a month. Real progress! This was a large school with forty-two students and each grade represented.

The years 1934-38 were the so called "Dust Bowl" years. Often times a storm would roll in and it was impossible to see across the schoolroom.

I made the decision not to turn students out in a "duster" without a parent or responsible party accompanying them. The decision came from a personal experience of being lost. I was crossing a field south of the schoolhouse to return to the place where I was boarding. After sometime I realized I had spent too long a time for I should have been home. It was after finding a fence and following it to the road that lead to my destination did I arrive there. Dust swept from that floor would have provided me with a productive farm had I had a place to put it!

There was little playground equipment and since there were several boys of good size, I asked if it would be possible to have a basketball goal. I had found out that some of the boys had been a bit rowdy during the year before - seemed they had to have a second teacher to finish the year. I hoped to get the energy channeled in another direction. It was agreed to provide my request. Cottonwood poles were cut from the nearby creek. The backboards were made from two by fours and one by twelve lumber. One board member, who later turned out to be my father-in-law, fashioned hoops from metal as he was an accomplished blacksmith. Basketball proved to be entertainment for the entire community. Boys, girls, and adults participated in games on Friday afternoons. The boys became proficient enough that they won a first and second place trophy at Atwood and Herdon tournaments. It was easier for them to shoot when in a building for they did not have to make adjustments for the wind. I have two trophies in my home as they were given to me upon my leaving the district at the end of the fourth year. It was at this school I found a wonderful wife and friend with whom I have spent 47 years.

In the fall of 1947, I returned to Fort Hays to finish my Bachelors degree, and the next fall began a thirty-one year teaching, coaching and finally elementary principalship at Oberlin Elementary School.

Upon retirement in 1979, I finished 37 years of a wonderful experience - working with the youth of Western Kansas!

****

Original Rock School or High Prairie, District #3 Atchison County
Photo submitted by Ralph Scholz, Huron, Kansas

Chapter Three

Low student enrollment and school closings were prevalent in the 1950's and 60's. If the enrollment dropped below 10 students, the school usually closed, and the children were sent to a neighboring school or into the town school. Farm children could see the advantages of the larger schools in town offering organized sports, band, and other extra curricular activities. They also saw a chance to socialize and be a part of a larger class rather than being in a class by themselves or with one other student. Parents often opted to send their children to the town school, even if their rural school still existed, in hopes their children would receive a more expanded curriculum. Other parents fought hard to keep their one-room school open, as they believed this was the best educational setting for their children.

The 1963 Unification Law was a legislative attempt to modernize school district structure in Kansas. It pleased no one at that time. "Opinions ranged from 'ineffectual' to 'fascistic'," according to George D. Keith, then Director of School Unification for the Kansas State Department of Public Instruction. He also states that in time Kansas people were proven wrong and came to realize the direct connection between adequate and fair state financial support of schools and the uniformity of school district organization.

The number of operating one-room schools in 1945 stood at 4,981 but dropped to 414 by 1964. Young farm families were moving to town, and the number of children in the rural communities decreased. The end of this type of educational setting was in sight.

Normal Training for teachers had been discontinued, and college credits or a college degree were now needed for Kansas certification. Life certificates issued in earlier years were still recognized. Improvements now common in the school building were electricity, telephones, and some schools installed indoor restrooms in a former cloakroom or entry way.

Dermot School in Morton County closed in 1990, and Kansas lost its last one-room school.

Evelyn Hank of Nortonville sums up the demise of the one room school:

> In its era, the one-room school met the needs of the community in which it existed. Its survival was doomed by changing times and ideas.
>
> "To every loss there is a gain, for every gain there is a loss." I felt a keen loss as I left the one-room school system. It was "One for all and all for one." That was the spirit that uniquely existed there.

Atchison County

From Teacher to County Superintendent

Gettie Repstine
Atchison, Kansas

Hawthorne School - 1942-45; Hopewell School - 1946-49; Shannon Hill - 1949-56; Lane - 1956-57; Camp Creek - 1957-59; Atchison County Superintendent of Schools - 1959-69

My first teaching in Kansas was at Hawthorne School, 1942-45. Then I went to Hopewell from 1946-49. I taught Shannon Hill from 1949-56. I stayed at Shannon Hill until I got my degree. I went three nights a week after school at Mount St. Scholastica, Atchison, from 5:00 to 9:00 p.m. I received my degree in 1956, and I earned $3200. I taught Lane School two years. That school closed, so I went to Camp Creek for three years. I had a basketball team that played Ivalee Robbin's team at Pardee School. When I was at Camp Creek, I would come home and milk 38 cows. My husband had died, and there was no one else to help.

I became County Superintendent in 1959. I held that position until 1969. Gladys Winzer wanted to quit, and there were only two of us teachers qualified, Nellie Millikan and me. Nellie wanted to go to Florida with her husband, so that left me. I waited until 11:00 a.m. to file. Gladys was getting nervous and thought she would have to stay. Some people griped that I was getting too much money, but if they had worked as hard as I did they would not think that.

I went to the Junior High in Effingham in 1969-70, and had the library and taught some English classes. I retired in 1970.

Camp Creek School Students in 1959; Gettie Repstine, Teacher

Institute for Atchison County Teachers, 1959
Gettie Repstine, County Superintendent in front

Remains of Shannon Hill School, Atchison County

Hawthorne School, Atchison County

An Atchison County Rural Basketball team, 1958 Dale Bodenhausen, Coach

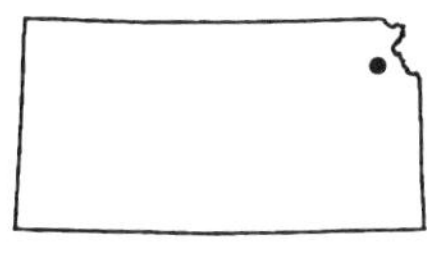
Atchison County

Teacher Loans Bra and Wins Championship

Emma Lou Mier Nieman
Nortonville, Kansas

Sunnyside School, Washington School, Clingan School. Pardee School

I was teaching at Sunnyside in Atchison County in 1955. We were playing for the County Championship Basketball trophy. Our team consisted of five boys and one tall, well developed girl. She didn't own a bra and didn't want to wear the team's T-shirt. We went in the restroom where I took off my bra, she wore it, and we won the championship trophy.

The parents were our best cheerleaders. I'll never forget one mother yelling at her son during the game. He was standing at the free throw line getting ready to throw the deciding point. She yelled, "Leroy, if you ever do anything for me, do it now!"

Pardee School, an inside view

What is left of Clingan School near Nortonville

Clingan School
Emma L. Mier Nieman, Teacher

My Car was Missing

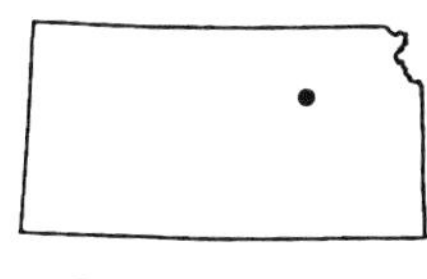

Geary County

Lois Cowan
Junction City, Kansas

Wetzel, District 9 - 1954-55 (named for Louis Wetzel, 1867)
Olson, District 11 - 1955-56; Pleasant Ridge, District 3 - 1956-57

I was a teacher, counselor, coach, and janitor. Wood, coal, and cobs had to be carried in after school, the fire banked and cleaning done. I still sneeze when I think of the dust scattered by the old broom. All this was done in readiness for the next day.

Christmas was the high point of the year with a large Christmas tree trimmed by homemade articles. Our program was by the teacher, parents and pupils. These were attended by the patrons of the district. We always had a big Christmas dinner and when I went to my car, I found it full of all those delicious goodies.

I suppose another highlight of my county teaching was giving a test to one of my students to go to Culver, a private school, and to know he scored very high. The Pleasant Ridge School had some of the richest people in the state and some of the poorest. These were the tenant farmers.

A time to remember was when my husband had purchased one of those small Opel cars. The first day I drove it to school it was very fascinating to the 8th grade boys. They begged me to let them drive. The school had ended for the day and my car had vanished! After extensive searching, I found it behind the outhouse. When the boys pushed it there, I will never know.

The Music Supervisor

Bernice Collins Dickson
Topeka, Kansas
Richland, Sunny Elevation, Capitol View and Union

Shawnee County
1956-57

My title was Music Supervisor for Shawnee County. There were six schools that I drove to once a week. One school, Richland, I remember was quite a distance. Each school paid me $40.00 for the four visits. That turned out to be a pretty good part-time job for a Washburn student.

I carried my portable 45 rpm record player with me as none of the schools had their own. We felt lucky to have a piano.

I remember being pregnant and trekking through snow to the outhouse. I remember how helpful and kind the regular teachers were to me. Probably grateful for some assistance, no matter how small.

What I remember best, however, was at Christmastime having to put on six different programs. The reason being, that this was a much-looked-forward-to social event. Parents and friends wanted to go to each other's programs.

The other thing that stands out in my mind, was that during rehearsals for the Christmas program, no matter how much or how loud the 7th and 8th grade boys sang, they never uttered one note at the performance - leaving the alto part entirely to me!

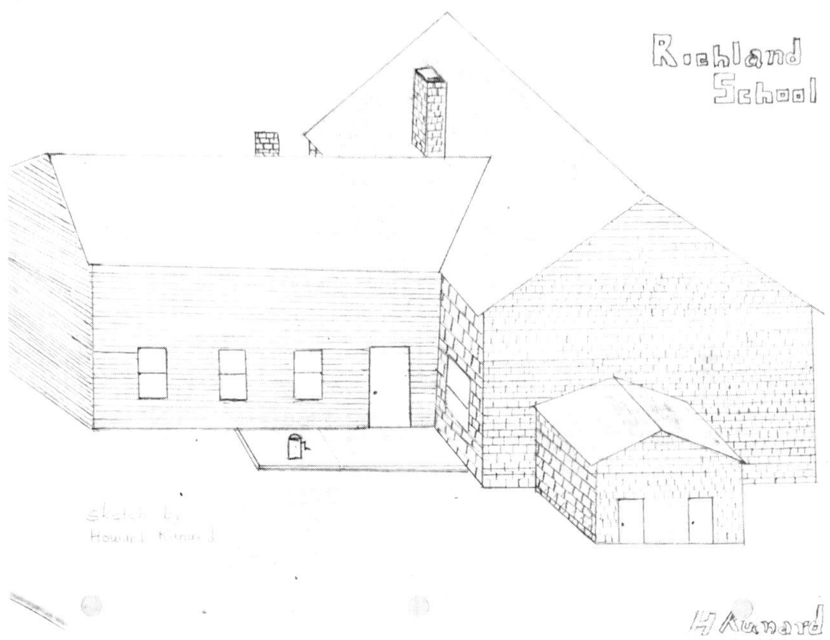

Richland School
Sketch by Howard Kunard

A Difference Between the 1940's and 1950's

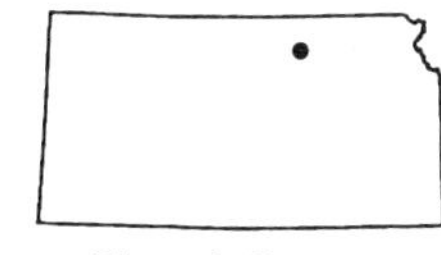

Cloud County

Gary Zabokrtsky
Topeka, Kansas

Huscher School, S.E. of Concordia - 1957-59

Teaching in a one room school in the late 1950's reminded me of my days as a student in one room schools during the mid 1940's. I taught at Huscher School southeast of Concordia, Cloud County from 1957-59.

Huscher consisted of a grain elevator, E.U.B. Church, two houses for the families of the elevator owner and minister and, of course, the schoolhouse.

The schoolroom had two cloak rooms on either side of the front entrance. On a cabinet were the crock water cooler, student cups and enamel wash pan. There was a raised platform or stage across the opposite end of the room.

The school yard had the usual swings, merry-go-round, ball diamond, flag pole, and two outhouses at the back of the property.

The school year was still eight months in length. Classes usually started on Labor Day or the day after, with the last day of school in mid-April.

The school day started at nine o'clock in the morning with dismissal at four o'clock in the afternoon. There was an hour for lunch and play time at noon, and fifteen minute recesses at mid-morning and mid-afternoon. Softball was the most popular activity.

During those two years enrollment ranged from about fifteen to eighteen students. At times there were students in all eight grades which meant that the class time for each grade level subject area averaged five minutes.

The school played an important part in community life. The patrons of the district met one evening each month for entertainment and refreshments. The students presented songs, dances and short skits three times during the year. The Christmas program remained the main event with the last day of school activities coming in a close second.

At Christmas time the school room was decorated with crepe paper streamers, seasonal bulletin boards and of course the traditional tree with student made decorations.

For the Christmas program, the front part of the classroom was separated from the rest of the room with curtains hung from a wire strung across the room. The students worked with vigor after Thanksgiving to prepare the scenery and props for the program. Of course, Santa appeared after the program and handed out gifts and sacks of candy, fruits and nuts, which were often stuck together.

On the last day of school the community would gather for a day of festivities. Before lunch the students would present a program. One year the students worked very hard to learn square dances. At noon the ladies would provide an ample basket dinner. The day ended with the traditional softball game.

Most of the teachers did not have college degrees and attended night and summer classes to renew their teaching certificates. The county superintendent supervised the schools and provided inservice for teachers. The main inservice was the "teacher's institute" which teachers attended for two or three days prior to the beginning of the school year. The superintendent would visit each school once a month. This was really a treat for the students as he would bring a movie projector and films.

Keith Trost, the County Superintendent, was a first cousin to over half of the students at Huscher.

One year Huscher School was responsible for organizing and hosting a track meet for the neighboring country schools. The usual individual team events were included. The township road crew graded the road for the running events. At noon the parents provided a basket lunch.

As I had attended one room rural schools in Washington County for six years, I was aware of the organization and day-to-day operation of the school. But there were some differences between the 40's and the 50's.

Teachers could no longer teach out of high school. There were electric lights, an electric motor on the water pump and a thermostat controlled oil heater. The former oil treated wood floor was covered with asbestos tiles. The horse barn out by the back fence was gone. During my second year at Huscher, the desks and attached seats, which were screwed in rows to wooden slat runners, were replaced with individual desks and chairs. One big advantage was a full basement which was a great place for recess during bad weather. Students raised a cloud of dust from the concrete floor when they roller skated.

With a declining rural population in the late 40's and 50's, the rural school districts were consolidated. Two, three or four districts merged and quite often one schoolhouse would be moved to a location near the center of the new district. The statewide school unification across Kansas in 1966 brought an end to an era which can never be brought back.

Gone forever are ice cream socials, monthly community gatherings, dust clouds from clapping together felt chalkboard erasers, recitation benches, desk ink wells, Kittle handwriting pads, gallon syrup buckets containing lunch, pictures of Washington, Lincoln and the "howling wolf" in a snowstorm, marching in the county fair parade, selling Christmas seals, purchasing saving stamps for war bonds, buckle overshoes lined up in front of the stove, sewing cards, world globe on a floor stand, slate chalkboards, green window shades, being the only one in your class, McCormick-Mathers English workbooks and playing Fox and Geese in the snow.

Unification, the Utopian Goal

Evelyn White Hank
Nortonville, Kansas

Atchison County

Lane School, Clingan School, Hickory Grove School

The teacher was highly respected in the community but not highly paid. My beginning salary at Lane School, District 35, was $50.00 per month for eight months.

The status quo of the rural school began to change after World War II. The enrollment was declining. The certification processes needed to be the same for all teachers. Normal Training was discontinued.

Unification became the utopian goal to solve the rural school problem.

The unification proponents were prepared with convincing arguments concerning the students, teacher and the citizens of the rural school districts.

For several years the Hickory Grove School was closed because of small enrollment. The school reopened when the number of school age children increased. Unification advocates pushed for a regulation that would eliminate the option of a district to reopen their school. This became an adopted policy. Many small enrollment schools were kept open in fear of extinction.

Many teachers were sold on the unification idea. They were convinced that a one or two grade lesson plan would give the teacher more time to help children with special needs. They also believed that children in low enrollment classes would profit with a competition incentive. I regard the self improvement incentive to be more realistic and rewarding. I was a lone student in my grade and I was a teacher of many single student classes.

Teacher qualification and salary became focused on college credits. Many valuable college courses were offered. There were also in my estimation, the "get-by-courses", which were of questionable value.

Unification proponents gave talks with figures and charts to show that this was a wise use of tax money. A school principal explained to me that money was wasted when it was spent to buy a teacher's desk copy for a grade level in which only one student was enrolled. But I knew textbooks were adopted for a five year period.

The one-room facility was a vulnerable target of the unification experts. A water system and restrooms were timely necessities. The two little outhouses located a distance from the schoolhouse were aptly assessed as outmoded. A water system was installed and the restrooms were built in the entry way while I was teaching Clingan School, District 38.

In its era, the one-room school met the needs of the community in which it existed. Its survival was doomed by changing times and ideas. I was privileged to be a part of that educational system as a student and a teacher.

"For every loss there is a gain,
For every gain there is a loss".

I felt a keen loss as I left the one-room school system. It was, "One for all and all for one." That was the spirit that uniquely existed there.

Lane School

The Last One-Room School in Kansas

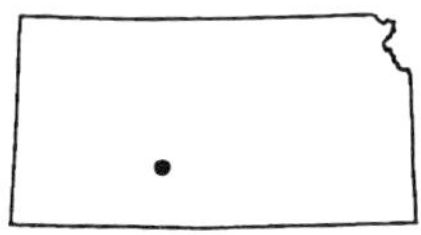

Selola Lewis

Rolla, Kansas

from an interview by Marjorie Retzlaff

Courtesy of Fort Hays State University

Morton County

Dermot School

1953-90

When I first came here, this school was called Antelope Valley. When they dedicated the new building they decided to call it Dermot because there used to be a Dermot school in the city of Dermot in Stevens County. No one around here remembers when it was a town.

I think the biggest benefit (of the one-room school) is they hear. I don't care how sophisticated and technical we get, learning is repetition. Some of the students are like sponges and absorb a lot. Ones that are slower, they hear it reinforced over and over and over. I think that is a benefit. Another benefit is they learn to tolerate younger ones. This is something they learn — to get along with all ages.

I have asked students who have gone on to college — "Now be honest with me. Has it (one-room school) hurt you?" They said they didn't think so. One of them said that out here they know there is so much to learn, because what they see the other kids learning. A lot of kids when they see just one grade they think they know a lot. Out here they realize there is lots to learn.

I intermix, like I have a gifted 6th grade boy, but I never thought of not calling on him if I wanted him to read with a 1st grader or a 2nd grader. Then I'll have a 2nd grader work with a 6th grader. That way if someone really needs it they aren't stigmatized. It's like a family in that we all help each other. I told them that always makes you stronger.

Happenings in a One-Room School

by Selola Lewis

I had made four snowmen out of chicken wire and covered it with cotton batting. Inside I put my first graders. One little fellow fell — he was like a turtle on his back — during the play I reached out and set him back on his feet and the play went on.

In one Christmas play a boy playing Santa came through the fireplace. This was fine during practice, but the night of the performance was a different story. The padded Santa suit was just too big for the fireplace and old Santa got stuck and pulled the fireplace over. It was good for laughs anyway.

One year we had only one girl. The play we wanted to do called for four girls, so three of our "all-American" boys agreed to dress up like girls — everyone joined in. The cook got grapefruits and really filled the boys out. We had a lot of fun. One man in the audience said, "I didn't know we had that many big girls."

On Halloween we had a masquerade. Anyone who wanted to dress up could. We had one gentleman in the community who usually came dressed as a woman. A group of men were visiting outside when in walked an ugly old witch who just nodded and went in to sit down. One of the men asked if it could be Bus and the others guessed that must be him. So the man went in and put his arm around the witch and gave her a pinch, then got up and left. He walked outside and who should walk up but Bus (not in costume) as he had just come from a meeting. Was the man's face red when he realized he had hugged and pinched his neighbor's wife. It was all in fun so they all had a good laugh.

During class one day a girl screamed — seems a salamander was walking toward her from the activity room. (He looked like a dinosaur to a small girl.) An older boy took him outside — don't know how he got in.

One hot day during the summer some of my supplies arrived. I opened the front door of the school and propped it open so I could carry boxes in, then decided to go ahead and put supplies away. When I went to close the door I heard a hiss — there was a snake caught in the door. I called my husband — he helped to removed the bull snake and let him go — bet he had a sore tummy.

Elections are held in our gym and I wanted the students to be unusually quiet and good that day. In science we were feeding Cam. I put in a cricket — the cricket jumped on my arm and the lizard went after it — I screamed, throwing the lizard on the floor. The boys rescued it and peace was restored — only one making a noise was the teacher.

Another Halloween an old lady (very well dressed) in black — complete down to girdle and hat with a veil fooled everyone — turned out to be an eighth grade boy who had dressed in his grandmother's good clothes.

After one program a few stayed to visit and clean up. Otis Lee Daniels sat at the piano. As he played the songs — little heads would perk up and they would come forward to do their song and then wander away as others came forward. The program after the program was as good as the original.

We needed basketball suits so the ladies and men in the community played a basketball game against each other. The men had to wear gloves and slippers. The ladies wore white shirts and red and white polka-dot bloomers. One older lady was the coach, and she dressed much like a witch and carried a skillet. We got the suits and a lot of fun was had by everyone.

One April Fool's day we were playing ball across the road from the school. Two younger boys were walking around. All at once John came running and yelling, "Johnny's been bit by a rattlesnake." I started to run and then said, "Oh, It's April Fool's." He said, "Shucks, we found a crooked stick. Looks like a snake." He went home and told his Dad about it — his Dad didn't think it was funny — because it was not uncommon to find rattlesnakes by the flag pole, under the jungle gym, you name it — one could be there.

The Dermot School closed with the retirement of Selola Lewis in 1990. This closing marked the end of one-room schools in Kansas.

Chapter Four

"Everything was built around the school. . . people, when they think about having a good time, they always think about school."

George D. Keith

Teachers and former students alike remember the good things about the one-room school and for the most part forget the negative aspects as they write down their memories.

Fred Wiley, now living in California, writes of his adventures while attending Riverside School near Lawrence in 1948:

> The order of events I am relating may be a bit hazy, but the facts are still real. The school had indoor bathrooms, one for the girls and one for the boys. The boys' bathroom amounted to one old potty that we all used simultaneously at a designated time of day. Although I don't remember the smell, it must have stunk because none of us could hit the pot. The stories of being able to do our business with such force that it would reach the heights of telephone poles outdoors abounded each day. Somehow manhood and the act of going potty were connected together.
>
> I do remember doing Math and multiplication tables at the board. It was usually a contest to see who could write all the times tables through nine times nine on the board first. The second thing I remember is penmanship. We used an Esterbrook fountain pen, which was a requirement, and that our parents must have gotten at a drug store. The pen would leak, smear, and everything else, but it was what we used. There was also an ink well on each desk. I don't really remember using ink wells. . .
>
> My classroom experience in this country school may not have been what you compare with the present classroom tech-

nology but basic learning was there - feel, taste, see, and hear; all the human senses were used to implant the learning experience in my brain. What more can one ask for?

Doris Harris Braunbeck of Topeka attended Lone Rock School located near Topeka. She remembers walking across a prairie hay pasture about two miles to get to school. She wrote the following memories:

> We all wore dresses to school — no jeans or slacks — only under your dress and they had to be taken off when you got to school. Most of us wore long cotton stockings with garters to keep our stockings up — in addition to underwear.
>
> Toward the end of the second year (attending Lone Rock) we were given commodities from the government or state. Beans, Beans, Beans! The teacher cooked them on the stove, and I still remember to this day of hating to smell beans cooking. There were navy beans, lima beans, pinto beans, you name it! I don't remember what she used to flavor the beans, probably some sort of meat from the people she stayed with.
>
> I wore dresses made out of chicken feed sacks when I entered school. When I graduated, my mom sold some old hens to buy me a suit.
>
> I look back today and remember all of those times, the good times and the bad, the hard and rough times and thank my lucky stars that I got to be a part of that era.

Maxine Fritts of Missouri has honored the Lone Star School of Bison, Kansas (near LaCrosse) by designing an original sampler. She sells the samplers at local craft shows with the history of the school typed on an attached card.

Lone Star School Sampler

Maxine Fritts Korte

Blue Springs, Missouri

I grew up on the Kansas prairie in the small town of LaCrosse during the Great Depression and dust storms. The Lone Star School, Bison, Kansas, was a country school about three miles east of LaCrosse. It was built around 1877. The German Methodist Church and School District #34 shared the Lone Star School from 1877 to 1890 until the Methodist congregation outgrew the school and built a larger church in Bison. In 1890 the Methodist Church sold the Lone Star building to the school district for $300.00. The building still stands and is maintained by a county extension group, the Sunshine Unit.

I dedicate this sampler to my native state of Kansas and to all the people who preserve our history.

Lone Star School, Bison, Kansas

The Teacher

Sent by Annie Irene Thompson Canady
Shawnee, Kansas

Write no poem men's hearts to thrill, no song I sing to lift men's souls; no battle front, no soldiers lead; in halls of state I boast no skill; I just teach school.

I just teach school. But poet's thrill, and singer's joy, and soldier's fire, and stateman's power - all, all are mine; I have all this whene'er I will, as I teach school.

The poets, soldiers, statesmen - all: I see them in the speaking eye, in face aglow with purpose strong, in straightened bodies, tense and tall, when I teach school.

And they, uplifted, gaze intent on cherished heights they soon shall reach. And mine the hands that led them on! If I inspired them, I'm content, and still teach school.

And when I see the world of men and know my touch has guided some, I ne'er regret a moment's toil; and if I'd have my choice again, I'd still teach school.

Copied

Teacher's Prayer

I want to teach my students how
To live life on this earth —
To face its struggles and its strife
And how to improve their worth —
Not just the lesson in a book
On how the river flows —
But how to choose the proper path
Wherever they may go —
To understand eternal truth
And know the right from wrong —
And gather all the beauty of
A flower and a song —
For if I help the world to grow
In wisdom and in grace —
Then I shall feel that I have won
And I have filled my place —
And so I ask your guidance, God
That I may do my part —
For character and confidence
And happiness of heart.

— *James J. Metcalf*

Index By Contributor

Index By County

Index By Schools

Index By Pictures

Bibliography

Kansas State Retired Teachers Association. Heritage of our Schools: The Pride of Kansas. Dodge City: Cultural Heritage and Arts Center, 1976.

Keith, George D. "Where Are We in School District Unification." Kansas Teacher November 1964: 17-19.

Gulliford, Andrew. America's Country Schools. Washington, D.C.: Preservation Press, 1984.

Loganbill, James. "The One-Room Schoolhouse." Kanhistique September 1984.

Phi Delta Kappa. Tales from the One-Room Schoolhouse. University of Kansas Kappa Chapter, Phi Delta Kappa, 1989.

Schlageck, John and Mace Thorton. "Ending an Era". Kansas Living Summer 1990: 13-15.